D1038991

Show Me *Your* GLORY

Show Me *Your* Glory

True Stories of Miracles

Bill Hart

© Copyright 2003 – Bill Hart
All rights reserved. This book is protected by the copyright laws of the United
States of America. This book may not be copied or reprinted for commercial gain
or profit. The use of short quotations or occasional page copying for personal or
group study is permitted and encouraged. Permission will be granted upon
request. Unless otherwise identified, Scripture quotations are from the New
King James Version of the Bible. Please note that Destiny Image's publishing
style capitalizes certain pronouns in Scripture that refer to the Father, Son, and
Holy Spirit, and may differ from some Bible publishers' styles.
Take note that the name satan and related names are not capitalized. We choose
not to acknowledge him, even to the point of violating grammatical rules.

Treasure House

An Imprint of

Destiny Image® Publishers, Inc.

P.O. Box 310
Shippensburg, PA 17257-0310

"For where your treasure is, there will your heart be also."
Matthew 6:21

ISBN 0-7684-2958-7

For Worldwide Distribution
Printed in the U.S.A.

This book and all other Destiny Image, Revival Press,
MercyPlace, Fresh Bread, Destiny Image Fiction, and
Treasure House books are available at Christian bookstores
and distributors worldwide.

1 2 3 4 5 6 7 8 9 10 / 09 08 07 06 05 04

For a U.S. bookstore nearest you, call
1-800-722-6774.
For more information on foreign distributors, call
717-532-3040.
Or reach us on the Internet:

www.destinyimage.com

Dedication

This book is dedicated to...

... my grandmother, Rachel Sterling, a godly woman who made Jesus real to me at a young age.

... my mother, Ruby, and late father, Houston.

... my loving wife, Sue.

... my son, David Hart, and his wife, Anna.

... my daughter, Jennifer, and her husband, Darren Shaw.

... my three wonderful grandchildren, Kendall, Samuel, and Nadia.

... and all the wonderful members of Cathedral of Praise.

Acknowledgments

Many thanks:

To my friend and fellow worker, Carla Kaufman, who worked so faithfully to bring this book to life.

To Donna Triplett, who has always believed in this ministry and encouraged this work.

To all the staff of Cathedral of Praise and KingsWay, who have taken the burden of labor from me, so that I could hear the voice of the Lord.

Most importantly, to the wonderful person of the Holy Spirit, who has faithfully manifested His presence these many years.

Endorsements

Bill Hart has been my friend since 1985. I've always called him "Wild Bill" because of his radical love for Jesus and his continuous desire to experience His glory. This book is definitely for those who are very hungry for God and not willing to settle for average.

Dr. Dale Gentry
Breakout Prayer Network

Pastor Bill Hart has touched the heart's cry of saints across the nations in his book, *Show Me Your Glory*. You will be stirred and motivated to seek the Lord on a much deeper level. You too will want to seek the smile of His face and the touch of His hand. As Bill shares his wonderful account of how he has encountered important aspects of the revealed glory of God, you will be blessed to see the hand of God upon his life opening doors of blessings. This book will be a blessing to all who are longing to seek the glory of God.

Bobby Conner
Demonstration of God's Power Ministries

If you are hungry for revival glory, if you are hungry for God's presence, you have in this book one of the greatest manuals to usher you into the reality of the anointing and glory of God. At various times throughout the book I experienced tears and laughter. Often I burst into worship, praying in the Spirit. I was refreshed, inspired, encouraged, and enlightened.

Mahesh Chavda
Senior Pastor, All Nations Church

Table of Contents

Foreword

Years ago while reading the Bible, I fell into a trance-like sleep. I was a Hindu teenager seeking answers for my life, reading about Jesus Christ in the New Testament on a humid night in Mombasa, Kenya. In this trance-like sleep, which lasted all night, I was in Heaven surrounded by the glory of God, and I met the King of Glory. At the conclusion of this experience I got on my knees and prayed to receive Jesus Christ as my Savior. I never looked back from that day. The two things that were imprinted on my heart from that experience were the eyes of the Lord, full of compassion, love, and joy, and the awesome effect of being in the glory of God.

I then came to the United States to attend university. One evening as a young college student, I attended Bill Hart's church in Lubbock, Texas. Suddenly the glory of God was manifested in that church as Bill Hart prayed. It was that same heavenly presence I had experienced years before that culminated in my receiving Christ as my Savior.

Over a quarter century, bonds of brotherly love and deep friendship have joined our hearts. But more than anything else, it's been our mutual love and passion for the presence of God. I know Bill Hart is a man who has experienced the manifest glory of God. Like me, he has been transformed by that glory. He has been a present-day pioneer on a journey to seek more of the reality of the presence of God.

If you are hungry for revival glory, if you are hungry for His presence, you have in this book one of the greatest manuals to usher you into the reality of the anointing and glory of God.

The secret that let Joshua and Caleb enter the Promised Land while the rest of their generation perished was the cloud of God's glory. Glory is the manifest presence of God in our midst. Bill Hart imparts wisdom keys to usher you into the glory. You will learn in these pages to become a worshiper who can be "*harpazo'd*" or catapulted into the presence of God.

At various times throughout the book I experienced tears and laughter. Often I burst into worship, praying in the Spirit. I was refreshed, inspired, encouraged, and enlightened. Revival will come as we learn about the glory and steadfastly continue in the cloud. This anointing can transform any and every life. I cannot wait for part two of this book. As Bill Hart would say, "I like it, I love it, I want some more of it." Lord, show us Your glory!

Dr. Mahesh Chavda
Senior Pastor, All Nations Church

Introduction

What a privilege that we live in a day that is the most exciting time in the history of the Church. The Bible tells of the days when God will restore His glory to His people. I believe that we are in those days spoken by the prophets of old. All over the earth, the Church is beginning to come alive with God's presence. This humble book is intended to stir faith in all who read it. Just imagine what will happen when the Church really begins to believe that He is the same yesterday, today, and forever.

The pages of this book detail the biblical accounts, since the days of Moses, of God revealing His glory to man. In the early 1970s, I personally encountered God's cloud of glory for the first time. There I discovered that the mysteries written of in the Old Testament—mysteries of the intimate relationship between Creator and man—are attainable today.

As you begin to read Chapter 2, I encourage you to abandon patterns of the past, your preconceived ideas, and any limitation that may hinder you from your own breakthrough into the "realm of glory." As you let go of these hindrances, a transformation awaits; it will empower you to walk in the same boldness and victory as did our "fathers of the faith."

Our heavenly Father ultimately desires to relate with His children "face-to-face." Sense yourself walking from the outer courts into the Holy of Holies as you contemplate Chapters 3 and 4. Allow the Holy Spirit to guide you into God's presence by utilizing the keys of prayer, praise, and worship.

I believe that once you encounter the uncompromising reality of the living God, you and I will share the same passion. Our united cry for this hour is, "Show Me Your Glory." You can return to His presence; believe that Chapter 5, "The Pathway to Glory," will give you direction along the way.

Rejoice and rest as you enjoy Chapters 6 and 7. The life of the true believer is an adventurous and joyful one. Continually remain focused on the strength of the great "I AM," and you will find that the journey is not for your sake alone, but for those lives you touch along the way. As you will read in Chapter 8, it is through the revealing of His true sons and daughters that the Kingdom of God will be seen upon the earth.

Methods that man has devised to reach the lost for Christ are lacking in power. Chapter 9, "Glory Evangelism," and Chapter 10, "The Glory Ministry," contain Scriptures that teach us how to successfully invoke the power of the Holy Spirit. His power is necessary to evangelize and minister in a lost and dying world.

The final chapter, "The Glory Prepares Us," will equip and encourage you to seek God and all the blessings He has planned for your life. Near the end, you will read of the transition of leadership from Moses to Joshua. God is calling you also to break out from the old and into the new. Are you ready to go to the next level? Are you prepared to transform from goodness to greatness? Once you experience God's glory, your life will never be the same.

CHAPTER 1

The Glory Cloud

"Repent therefore and be converted, that your sins may be blotted out, so that times of refreshing may come from the presence of the Lord" (Acts 3:19). Where do the times of refreshing come from? They come from the presence of the Lord. Lay hold of this revelation of truth and impress that deep within your mind: The times of refreshing come from the presence of the Lord.

We must be diligent to pursue the presence of God. Now you may ask, "How do we pursue the presence of God? Doesn't His presence pursue us?" It's true that God is omnipresent, but we must train ourselves to be constantly aware of His presence and become those who run diligently after God.

Wouldn't it be wonderful if every time you went to church everything was totally conducted and orchestrated by God? Imagine not a taint of striving flesh in the service, or any human initiative involved, but simply man agreeing with what God was doing. True revival begins when God's presence is manifested in the midst of the church. This sets the stage for the miraculous to happen, and then the Lord will add to the church daily those who would be saved.

Revival is destined to break out because in the presence of God every need is met. Now granted, God does use His people to meet needs, but that's only part of the fruit of His presence. God's people obediently meet the needs of others simply as a result of being exposed to His abounding love and generosity.

We can find many Scriptures in the Old Testament about the "glory cloud." If you've ever been aware of the cloud of glory, then you know that being engulfed in His glory is the single most significant event that could ever happen to you. There is something about human nature that when we look towards the sky, we all want to go up into the clouds.

Clouds can symbolize a place of peace and rest, a place of escape. They also can symbolize a place of victory because the cloud is high above the earth's troubles. Calm clouds appear so cool, peaceful, and pleasant. Unfortunately, if you were to go up in the middle of one, you would find that natural clouds can be deceiving. If you were a pilot, you wouldn't choose to fly into the middle of clouds unless you had no other alternative.

Initially, the cloud of God is similar because when you first encounter God's cloud, it can bring great tribulation to your life. If you were to fly through a thunderstorm, as I have before, you would experience great turbulence and stress to the plane. In fact, if you did not trust the way the plane was engineered, you'd think it was going to fall apart. Have you ever felt like your plane was going to break apart and you wondered, *How do the wings stay on?*

Likewise, when we come into God's presence and begin to have a personal encounter with the Lord, He stretches us and causes stress to all our weak spots. Hebrews 12:26b-27 says, " 'Yet once more I shake not only the earth, but also heaven.' Now this, 'Yet once more,' indicates the removal of those things that are being shaken, as of things that are made, that the things which cannot be shaken may remain."

And so it is with us. When we initially enter into God's presence, God deals with our life. Where there is sin, it will be exposed. If there is fear or anxiety or unbelief or idolatry, it will be dealt with because God will reveal the things in your life that are causing you defeat. The sense that something must be dealt with in our lives is called the conviction of the Holy Spirit. Jesus said in John 16:8, "When He [the Holy Spirit] has come, He will convict the world of sin, and of righteousness, and of judgment." Thank God, He does.

Without the conviction of the Holy Spirit, we would remain in constant turmoil. The Holy Spirit continuously exposes the sin in our hearts so that the heart can be cleansed and become a holy place where the glory can dwell. In the Old Testament, they struggled to provide a place of abiding for the Lord. In order to accomplish their task, they had to follow very strict guidelines for building the temple that would house the ark of the covenant. God gave the people specific instructions to help them prepare a holy habitation for His glory.

We know that in the new covenant, the temple is not something that's built with the hands of men. Today, we don't construct physical buildings to prepare for the glory. Instead, the Bible tells us that we, ourselves, are the temples of the Holy Spirit (see 1 Cor. 3:16). We are the dwelling place of God. When the Holy Spirit is manifesting in our church services, it isn't because He comes in from the side door, but He reveals Himself in and through us.

No longer is man circumcised outwardly to show his faith, to prove he's a covenant child; but the circumcision takes place in the heart, and it is there that God desires to dwell. God no longer instructs us through the priests in the outward temple, but the Holy Spirit, who builds the temple within us, now teaches us. The old covenant is symbolic of what God is doing in the new. Just as there had to be exact specifications for building the outward temple, there are also specific plans and designs for the inward temple that God is building in us. He is erecting a holy place for His Spirit to dwell, establishing His Son Jesus Christ as the chief cornerstone. "Coming to Him as to a living stone, rejected indeed by men, but chosen by God and precious, you also, as living stones, are being built up a spiritual house, a holy priesthood, to offer up spiritual sacrifices acceptable to God through Jesus Christ" (1 Peter 2:4-5).

As we study Exodus chapter 19 and learn more about the cloud of glory, we can get somewhat of a sense of how God operates. His mode of operation hasn't changed; it's just that now God no longer deals with the external but with the internal. We can see the importance of the glory of God when the Lord was speaking to Moses. Verse 9 says, " 'Behold, I come to you in the thick cloud, that the people may hear when I speak with you, and believe you forever.' So Moses told the words of the people to the Lord." So the Lord manifested Himself in the cloud.

Unless the Word is accompanied by God's glory, we will be unable to hear what the Spirit is saying. Therefore, when the people in the church come together, we need to pray, "Lord, Holy Spirit, come and be manifested so we can hear you—hear the voice of the Father." Jesus said in John 16:13-14, "When He, the Spirit of truth, has come, He will guide you into all truth; for He will not speak on His own authority, but whatever He hears He will speak; and He will tell you things to come. He will glorify Me, for He will take of what is Mine and declare it to you."

The Holy Spirit comes as a cloud and in the atmosphere of the cloud we hear the voice of God. Exodus 19:16 says, "Then it came to pass on the third day, in the morning, that there were thunderings and lightnings, and a thick cloud on the mountain; and the sound of the trumpet was very loud, so that all the people who were in the camp trembled."

The role of the pastor is to simply introduce people to God. My responsibility as a pastor is not to do anything but to say, "This is the way, walk you in it," or "Come to this pasture, you can dwell here," or "The door is open, enter in." My job or an elder's job is not to supply you with everything you need, but to bring you to the source of the supply.

In the old order of churches with which I was formerly associated, pastors were treated like hirelings. The pastor was the one you would call if you needed groceries delivered to your house. If you needed this or that done, you would contact him. The pastor was expected to be everyone's servant. But that's not the pastor's responsibility.

Acts 6:4 says, "But we will give ourselves continually to prayer and to the ministry of the word." What were the responsibilities of the apostles, prophets, teachers, and pastors? They were to find the cloud and make sure that the cloud was in the house. Every time they came together in the Book of Acts, the glory of God was manifested, not only in the house but also all over Jerusalem.

Acts 6:1 reveals that murmuring arose in the camp because the widows' needs weren't being met. So the apostles appointed deacons as servants, and those deacons began to meet the temporal needs in the Christian community. But in American churches, pastors have often been relegated to the ministry of a deacon. Their performance is judged by their administrative skills, their ability to organize committees, their ability to work with deacon boards, and other services that have nothing whatsoever to do with the ministry of a pastor. Pastors aren't called to do those things; pastors are spiritual men. They are to lead the flock into the glory cloud.

You don't attend church services to conduct business meetings, cast votes on the most pressing issues of the day, or to listen to the pastor tell you about the church's new programs and how they will enhance your life. The only thing that will really enhance your life is the cloud of glory. When we enter the house of God, our focus and purpose should be worshiping the Lord and entering into His gates of glory.

Anytime God spoke to Moses the cloud was evident. Programs in the church may flow and be abundant, but they all have to come forth out of the glory that is sent from above and not below. That which is birthed below is demonic and sensual and earthly; that which is from above is from God. All good gifts that remain come from God above.

> *Then the Lord said to Moses, "Come up to Me on the mountain and be there; and I will give you tablets of stone, and the law and commandments which I have written, that you may teach them." So Moses arose with his assistant Joshua, and Moses went up to the mountain of God. And he said to the elders, "Wait here for us until we come back to you. Indeed, Aaron and Hur are with you. If any man has a difficulty, let*

him go to them." Then Moses went up into the mountain, and a cloud covered the mountain. Now the glory of the Lord rested on Mount Sinai, and the cloud covered it six days. And on the seventh day He called to Moses out of the midst of the cloud. The sight of the glory of the Lord was like a consuming fire on the top of the mountain in the eyes of the children of Israel (Exodus 24:12-17).

The glory comes as a consuming fire that purifies the heart of man. There are Christians in various camps who resist the fire and preaching that will upset them. But God is a consuming fire! God will burn out the dross and the chaff. He'll burn out the arrogance and the pride of man. Fire symbolizes purity, and God wants to bring purity into our hearts so our motives are right. He wants us to have a right spirit, a right attitude, a right heart, and a right desire.

It doesn't mean we are able to be perfect at all times. We cannot make ourselves righteous. But we have to present ourselves to the Righteous One and allow Him to deal with our very core. And the glory will deal with you. If you find yourself wanting to stay away from the house of God, it's an indication that you're trying to hide your heart. If there's an urgent desire in you to run to the mountain, knowing that when you get there God will burn out the impurities, then you know you're on the right track.

The sight of the glory of the Lord was like a consuming fire on the top of the mountain in the eyes of the children of Israel. So Moses went into the midst of the cloud and went up into the mountain. And Moses was on the mountain forty days and forty nights (Exodus 24:17-18).

Is it any wonder that when he came off the mountain his hair had changed color and his face was shining? He had spent 40 days and 40 nights enveloped in the cloud of glory.

Something about the cloud will transform your life. When you get in the presence of the Lord, change takes place. You go in one side as one kind of man and you come out the other side completely different. It's like going through God's holy car wash: in one way and out another. Have you ever driven a really dirty car until you couldn't stand it any longer, and then you had it washed? It was like a whole different car! You knew it was the same car, but now it had a brand-new appearance.

That's the way it happens with us when we encounter God. We know we're in the same body and have the same mind, but suddenly everything seems entirely new. When we pass through the glory of God, He burns away the dross and chaff and brings cleansing to our lives in the midst of His presence.

Thus we have the reason not to forsake the assembling of ourselves together; we're to come together and worship the Lord. In fact, the Book of Acts says that the early Christians met in the temple—daily. I believe there will come a day when that desire will be restored. The day will come when we get off work and instead of driving straight home, we'll first drive to the church.

Right now when we get off work we might say, "Well, I can't wait to get home and get in front of the television to watch the evening news!" Instead, you'll be saying, "I can't wait to get to the house of God! I'm going to have to talk to my boss about going in 30 minutes early and getting off 30 minutes early because I want to be there at the beginning of the service. I don't want to miss a thing!"

In these daily meetings we'll come in every evening and bathe in the glory together. Acts 2:42 says, "And they continued steadfastly in the apostles' doctrine and fellowship, in the breaking of bread, and in prayers." And it wasn't just a few of them who gathered a couple of mornings a week; it was the whole body, and it continued daily.

Can you imagine what will happen when the entire body is committed to offering themselves to the presence of God on a continual basis? That's how revival breaks loose! If we want to see revival in our city or town, it won't come simply because we show up and look nice. It won't come because we have attained it by works. Revival will come because we have continued steadfastly in the presence of the Lord.

I first experienced His glory cloud in the early 70s in the church I pastored in Lubbock, Texas. During that time, many men in the church would gather several nights a week to seek the presence of the Lord. Early one morning during that season of prayer, we were made aware of God's presence in such a mighty way that our lives were changed forever. Our hearts were laid bare as He was manifesting in our midst!

The very next week in the Sunday night service something happened that would also alter my life forever and the lives of all who were present. During the invitation at the end of service, I was standing on the platform and the congregation that numbered about 60 people were standing facing me. At that moment I witnessed the visible Cloud of Glory enter the back of the sanctuary.

The Cloud began to move toward the front of the church, and as He passed each of those standing, he or she would collapse into the pews or onto the floor. Everyone who was there that night was baptized in the Holy Spirit, and those who were sick were healed. It was the most awesome demonstration that I have ever witnessed. That miraculous move of God started something that lasted several months.

The glory of God was so evident that if you were to enter the church even when there weren't any services in session, you would have to crawl to the front of the sanctuary. The weight of glory was there, and it was like experiencing open-heart surgery. People were driving hundreds of miles just to be in the presence of the Lord. The gifts of the Spirit were so pronounced and accurate that there wasn't any doubt that they were inspired by Heaven. The hunger that was created out of that encounter still lives in the hearts of all who experienced it.

The Spirit will always come before the works, and the works will always follow the Spirit. When the anointing begins to flow, we'll find ourselves attending our churches on a daily basis. The Holy Spirit will begin to gather us, and He will draw us into the house of the Lord. It will not be something that man will have to strive to build up.

God abhors the flesh and how it tries to manufacture the glory. Don't you know the Lord has been grieved with how man has made light of the glory of God over the years and tried to mix the flesh in it? When I'm preparing to preach, I tell the Lord, "I'm not going to do a single thing to try and make something happen. I'll respond obediently to Thy will."

You can't sit around waiting for God to move you, but you also shouldn't try to manufacture the anointing of God. That's the resolve of my heart. I say, "Lord, even if the church service is a flop, I'm not going to get in there and pump it up to make it look better. If it flops, then it's Your flop, God—not mine. And if it succeeds, it's Your success—not mine."

I have often had people run to me in a panic mode saying, "What are you going to do about this, or what are you going to do about that?" And I'll say, "I don't know; I'm not God. Ask Him what He's going to do about it." Now if God wants me to do something about it, and He impresses on me to be His instrument, I'll be glad to oblige. But until that happens, don't talk to me; talk to Him.

People say, "I've been talking to Him." And my answer is, "Well, maybe you should pray to hear more clearly." There is a good example to illustrate my point. A young man may approach a girl and boldly proclaim, "God told me I'm going to marry you." Well, maybe God had told him that, but he would be wise to let God first speak to her too. She may not think God is saying the same thing to her. She might think she is hearing God say, "See that other boy over there..."

We need to begin by praying in one accord in order to hear accurately what the Spirit is saying. We are able to reach this unity by abiding in the presence of God together. As we pray and begin waiting, watching, and listening, the Spirit of truth will come. Jesus said in John 16:13, "However, when He, the Spirit of truth, has come, He will guide you into all truth; for He will not speak on His own authority, but whatever He hears He will speak; and He will tell you things to come." Thank God, He's a revealer.

I feel like a little child at times because I'm just now beginning to learn what my spiritual world is about. If we watch a baby learn how to walk, we see him fall down many times. He makes a lot of mistakes as he grows. I can relate these same feelings to my relationship with my heavenly Father and confess, "Lord, I feel like a child, not really knowing how to walk in Your ways, just stumbling along. Sometimes I get it right, sometimes I don't." Thank God for His grace.

Many parents are not patient with their children. Sometimes we punish children even when they are trying their best to learn. The Lord has more patience with us than earthly parents have with their very own children. He is longsuffering with us. If we would only be as longsuffering as God is, it would cure a lot of the problems in the world.

So the Lord is looking upon the Church now and saying, "You have accomplished many things and you are learning to run and not faint. Don't give up now because you will succeed if you keep on trying." We learn how to walk until finally it's not laborious at all; it becomes totally natural. It's the same with learning to flow in the Spirit. In time we learn to cease from our struggling as we begin to enter into His rest. God Himself takes over and we become transformed by His presence.

In Exodus 33:7-9, we see the absolute dependence of the children of Israel on God's glory. They had no choice but to follow the Lord. It says,

Moses took his tent and pitched it outside the camp, far from the camp, and called it the tabernacle of meeting. And it came to pass that everyone who sought the Lord went out to the tabernacle of meeting which was outside the camp. So it was, whenever Moses went out to the tabernacle, that all the people rose, and each man stood at his tent door and watched Moses until he had gone into the tabernacle. And it came to pass, when Moses entered the tabernacle, that the pillar of cloud descended and stood at the door of the tabernacle, and the Lord talked with Moses (Exodus 33:7-9).

I cherish the times when I'm alone and God comes and talks with me. Do you realize that you can have an intimate conversation with God Himself if you're in His presence?

All the people saw the pillar of cloud standing at the tabernacle door, and all the people rose and worshiped, each man in his tent door. So the Lord spoke to Moses face to face, as a man speaks to his friend. And he would return to the camp, but his servant Joshua the son of Nun, a young man, did not depart from the tabernacle....."Now therefore, I pray, if I have found grace in Your sight, show me now Your way, that I may know You and that I may find grace in Your sight. And consider that this nation is Your people." And He said, "My Presence will go with you, and I will give you rest" (Exodus 33:10-11,13-14).

Then Moses responds in verses 15-16,

"If Your Presence does not go with us, do not bring us up from here. For how then will it be known that Your people and I have found grace in Your sight, except You go with us? So we shall be separate, Your people and I, from all the people who are upon the face of the earth" (Exodus 33:15-16).

What would the condition of the Church in America be today if that would have been our cry all along? Imagine if we had said, "Lord, we don't want to go anywhere without Your leadership; we don't want to do anything apart from Your glory. We want to be utterly dependent upon You."

Moses was willing to sacrifice the whole nation if it meant God would not be with them. He was willing to say, "Forget it, we'll die out here." That takes quite a commitment, doesn't it? "Lord, if You don't go with us, then we'll just die here."

That's the kind of commitment that many of the people and I made when we started our church. We told the Lord that we didn't want just another church; we wanted something special. We wanted the glory of God in our midst. We didn't want to compare ourselves with other churches, or with any other people. We continue to tell the Lord, "We are looking to You to be our example, oh God. Continue to lead us by Your Spirit."

We cannot judge success by our own standards. We must look to the Lord and simply refuse to be found in the place of judgment, but rather in the place of rest. When you are in the place of judgment, you are always in a place of great conflict because you are constantly evaluating and either putting down or lifting up. But in a place of rest there is no judging. If we rest in the cloud, we will cease from all strife and find His perfect peace. When the Holy Spirit leads us, He leads us beside still waters and restores our soul.

When the nation of Israel made their way through the wilderness, they had to depend on the Lord. God is also saying to us, "I want you to be dependent on Me." Will we be dependent on the Lord? Will we die to self? Do you know what it means to be solely dependent upon the Lord? It means that you do not let yourself rule, but you say, "I'm going to let God rule."

When self rules, it produces death. But what happens when God rules? You receive righteousness, peace, and joy. You cannot buy those gifts with money. You cannot put a price tag on the riches in glory, but you can surely count the costs when there is no glory.

The enemy will extract everything from your life. He will destroy all that you hold precious. He'll rob you of your relationships; he'll steal your inner peace and joy, and blindside your faith because he comes to steal, kill, and destroy.

When the glory comes, the abundance of God is poured out upon your life for He has come to give you life, and to give you life more abundantly. Thank God that we are serving that kind of God. In John 14:1-2 Jesus said, "Let not your heart be troubled; you believe in God, believe also in Me. In My Father's house are many mansions [dwelling places]; if it were not so, I would have told you. I go to prepare a place for you." (Some translations say "mansions," not "dwelling places"; however, "mansions" is an incorrect translation.)

It goes on to say in verse 3, "And if I go and prepare a place for you, I will come again and receive you to Myself; that where I am, there you may be also."

Now, I want to tell you something that may challenge your theology. The above passage is not a funeral message; it's a right-now message. Jesus Christ has come again in the power of the Holy Spirit to bring you to the place of dwelling in the Father's house. That is not a futuristic word, saying, "When we all get to Heaven...." Jesus has prepared a place for you *today*, and you can live there in the here and now.

Jesus didn't say, "I'm going to come again and take you off somewhere." He said, "I'm going to come again and receive you to Myself." And where is Jesus? He's here, right now; and He's promised that where He is, you will also be. That confirms the rest of the Word of God. The Word of God is not confirmed by one passage; it's confirmed line upon line, precept upon precept. The Word is confirmed over and over again, and the Spirit gives the Word life.

Jesus simply meant that He will dwell among His people and bring them into an abiding place, a place prepared for them, a haven of refuge in the midst of a troubled world. God will give you an island in the midst of the storm. He'll harbor you in His Kingdom amidst the earthly kingdom that is ruled by satan.

> *Do you not know that you are the temple of God and that the Spirit of God dwells in you? If anyone defiles the temple of God, God will destroy him. For the temple of God is holy, which temple you are* (1 Corinthians 3:16-17).

Put up a flag and say, "This is the Kingdom of God and all who violate this place will be persecuted, for no harm shall come near Thy dwelling place." Let His Kingdom and dwelling place be established in you.

CHAPTER 2

The Realm of Glory

We were created to live in the glory, and today we are standing at a pivotal place in time where the Lord is saying, "I will once again manifest Myself to you." It is a radical departure when we leave the lifeless religion that many of us have known while growing up and begin to move into the miraculous supernatural realm. In that realm, God is continually creating new life. We know that the letter of the law kills, but the Spirit of the Lord gives life.

The anointing, or unction of God, comes to carry us into a new and excellent place. The Holy Spirit takes us as we are, nurtures us, and then transforms us into overcomers who walk boldly in His Kingdom. Unless we are walking in the Spirit, we will not have quality of life. Abundant life comes by following after the Spirit of God.

We make an exciting discovery when we abandon self and surrender into the next realm, for we are then positioned to be transported into something fresh, something new. The Lord said in Isaiah 65:17, "For behold, I create new heavens and a new earth; and the former shall not be remembered or come to mind."

We know the only one who can bring renewal in our lives is the Spirit of the Lord. Everything else that we possess produces results that are void of eternal rewards. Not only does the Spirit give us eternity, but He also brings unique insight and discernment such as we have not been capable of knowing in our flesh.

If we are going to become a Kingdom upon the earth, then we must become a people who have keen insight. I don't know about you, but I need a lot of help getting out of the way and letting God place me where He wants me to be. It is only through Him that I can be transported to the path that God wants me to walk on. There is an ultimate victory that God has for each one of us that will cause us to triumph in every area of life.

Did you know the Lord is interested in you obtaining victory? And victory comes to those who learn to walk in the Spirit, for they shall be called the sons of God. And as a son, you are a legal heir who is entitled to inherit all that the Father has promised to His children.

Not everyone who claims to be a Christian is a son; we are recognized only as sons by our spiritual walk. We mature through discipline and obedience. We also allow the Spirit to lead us into an intimate relationship with our Father. Add all these ingredients and this is what makes up the sum total of a son. Our sonship grants us legal rights and authority, and we hold a privileged position as we stand before God. We have, as His sons and daughters, inherited the generous riches and blessings of our heavenly Father.

In Second Corinthians chapter 3, we find the New Testament revelation that unfolds the glory that God wants to share. From the very beginning of time, it has been God's intention to manifest His glory to His people, and we learn that throughout the Scripture in the Old Testament there were many manifestations of glory. At times it was called the *shekinah*, which means the "presence of the Lord with us, dwelling among His people."

An exciting fact that we learn in the Old Testament is that the *shekinah* would often come as a cloud. In our church we have seen the cloud of glory and the presence of the Lord such as they witnessed in the days of the old covenant. It became the central goal of their lives to come to the place where God would manifest Himself in their midst, and that became the difference between those who were approved of God and those who were not.

Moses carried godly authority and revelation, not because he was born a great leader, but because he abided in the presence, the *shekinah* of the Lord. When he would go out to the place of meeting, the cloud would descend; and there in the midst of the cloud God would talk to him face to face. There were times when Moses was separated from his brethren because he was the one whom God called up to the mountain to receive revelation.

Time went by and Joshua, the son of Nun, and Caleb, also began to walk in the same *shekinah* presence of the Lord. God would manifest Himself to them, similar as He had to Moses, and they would stay in His presence. The longer they tarried, the more of God's nature was imparted to them. As they became more like God, they encompassed greater strength to overcome the enemy, sharper ears to hear the voice of the Lord, and swifter steps to run with the Spirit.

The glory came, not just as a thrill for them, but as a substantial part of their lives. They became dependent upon His glorious presence. I think God has that designed for the Church today. He wants to bring us to a place of total dependence. The greater your dependence upon the glory, the greater the potential is for achieving victory in your life.

That means that we must throw down our crutches and begin leaning on the everlasting arms. It is easy to lean upon the arm of the flesh. It is also easy to trust in our natural mind with its understanding, wisdom, and intellectual capability. But those things will profit us little.

We must remove our security nets that have made us comfortable and venture out to find that which God has for us. Transition is the event that leads up to a radical transformation. It is very difficult to make a transition from the flesh to the Spirit. The New Testament revelation of this change is the manifestation of the cross. The cross becomes the transitional place by which we make the conversion from the flesh to the Spirit. It is only through the cross, the death that Christ suffered there, and our identification with His death, that we can translate from the flesh to the Spirit.

When Jesus came, He said, "Most assuredly, I say to you, unless one is born of water and the Spirit, he cannot enter the kingdom of God" (Jn. 3:5). He is saying that you must come out of that which you were, in order to begin walking in the new realm of the Kingdom.

Our primary goal is to have Christ's Kingdom manifested within our life. Christians are to arrive at the place that His Kingdom is being revealed within us so that when the world sees us, they see His Kingdom. They won't be able to focus on who we are, or what we've been, but they will see only the hope of His calling in our life. They will see the manifestation of His love, His joy, and His peace being revealed through us. They will witness the heart of God manifested in their midst.

Isaiah is a book of the Kingdom. Chapter 60, verse 1 says, "Arise, shine; for your light has come! And the glory of the Lord is risen upon you." Out of that manifestation of glory comes a great harvest. The Word says that His people will begin to be drawn to and stream to the glory. In the last days the Church is not going to be built by the ingenuity, the intellect, or the wisdom and doctrine of man. The Church will be built by the glory of God.

The Lord said in Psalm 127:1, "Unless the Lord builds the house, they labor in vain who build it." That doesn't mean as we build it; it means as He builds it. And He can build it only by the revelation of His Son in our midst.

The Church is destined to go through a radical transformation. First we will embrace a totally different mind-set and go through a paradigm shift before God fulfills His plans upon the earth. His Kingdom will not come because we have learned to cross our "t's" and dot our "i's". God will establish His reign on earth as we seek His face and as He manifests Himself in our midst.

God will accomplish His will in the Body of Christ, but not because the Church has devised a system to achieve certain results. That may work fine in the natural, but man's methods only produce natural results. The true victory comes by the presence of the Lord breaking forth onto the scene.

When Jesus came, there was a radical breakthrough on the earth. The righteous Jews and Pharisees at the time were keeping the law as best they could. They had studied the law inside and out and were systematically following the pattern of what they knew in the old covenant in order to achieve righteousness.

And then, a prophetic event unfolded before their eyes according to the very Scriptures they studied. Jesus Christ came on the scene and broke down all the laws they had depended on, which they believed would bring them into a right standing with God. They did not realize that all they had been taught was simply to bring them to the revelation of the manifestation of God's glory.

We get caught up in the religion of the system and begin to think that religion is the ultimate goal. But the goal of the system or religion or doctrine is to lead us to the place that those things pass away when the greater things come. Jesus did not come to abolish the law; He came to fulfill it. Jesus was such an unexpected manifestation that they could not comprehend or accept Him. So they rejected the very cornerstone they were waiting for. They rejected the Holy One of Israel because they were locked into the pattern of the past.

Are you locked into the pattern of the past? If you are, you are destined to repeat the pattern until it fails. The arm of the flesh will achieve a certain goal, but the Spirit of the Lord will propel you beyond the limitations you set for yourself. I do not want to be limited by what I can do; I want what He can do in my midst.

Often in our attempt to break through to the glory of God, we do not have a true sense of reaching that goal. Most who do achieve a breakthrough to the glory and the victory of the Lord seldom recognize the extent of the breakthrough in which they have attained. God will not allow us to rest in a place of satisfaction until His Kingdom is fully manifested in our midst.

What God will deem the greatest successes upon the earth will appear to man to be the greatest of failures. That is evidenced in what the Bible says in First Corinthians 1:27: "But God has chosen the foolish things of the world to put to shame the wise, and God has chosen the weak things of the world to put to shame the things which are mighty." God chooses the lame, the maimed, and the blind—the base things of this world— to confound the wise.

In the last days, the greatest glory will not come out of any place you are expecting; it will come out of the caves, just as it did when David and his mighty men were hiding from the strong arm of Saul. The glory could be found in those caves. The glory was in the hidden places, in the things that the world could not see.

And it is exactly where the glory is today. The glory is coming through vessels we would not have expected. God will come out of obscure places like Bethlehem and a little manger. When Jesus came, they said, "How could this man be who He thinks He is and who they say He is? He is simply a carpenter out of Nazareth."

They were confounded as He spoke, and they asked, "Is this not Joseph's son?" They were amazed at His teaching, for His message was with power and authority. Jesus did not have the extent of religious teaching from the synagogue as the scribes and Pharisees had, yet when the words fell from His lips He imparted life and made the crowds marvel.

Preaching and teaching only the knowledge that you have attained from an intellectual standpoint will impart the law which Scripture tells us produces death. Second Corinthians 3:3 and 6 says, "Clearly you are an epistle of Christ, ministered by us, written not with ink but by the Spirit of the living God, not on tablets of stone but on tablets of flesh, that is, of the heart....sufficient as ministers of the new covenant, not of the letter but of the Spirit; for the letter kills, but the Spirit gives life."

You must preach and teach out of the Spirit, even if it seems to you that what you are saying is confusing. It is better to speak words of jibberish that you don't understand, but that God and the people understand, than it is to try to confound someone with carnal wisdom.

That is why the apostle Paul said in First Corinthians 2:4, "And my speech and my preaching were not with persuasive words of human wisdom, but in demonstration of the Spirit and of power."

Paul had the ability to get up and confound the wise with his great intellectual abilities. He was known as one of the greatest teachers of his day. But yet, when he stood to preach, he became a man who was frightened to use his natural talent and he simply said, "God, You must manifest or nothing will happen." He threw away his crutches. He said, "I want God's glory, I want God's glory, I want God's glory."

What set Israel apart was not the fact that they were better looking or a more astute people. It was not that they were a more socially accepted race. They were none of these. What set them apart from the other nations was the presence of God's glory. The cloud enshrouded the mercy seat that sat upon the ark of the covenant that abided with the Israelites. This is what separated the nation from all others. The glory separates and differentiates us and must abide in us, or we are no different than the rest of the world.

The disciples said, "Lord, where else could we go? You are the glory." Moses saw the glory of the Lord; and when he did, his face was transformed. He was transformed. And once the glory comes to you, you will never be the same. The anointing will destroy all that your flesh is trying to accomplish and will teach you to solely depend on the power of God.

The mercy seat in the ark of the covenant was a special place where God would rest His glory. In this hour, as the glory is coming, we are finding such mercy and compassion, and such love and understanding and joy. The key for us is to say, "Lord, this is the hour of the glory." And if the glory is coming, it must also be the hour of the Kingdom. God does not manifest His glory without a very specific reason. We have been taught to pray, "Thy Kingdom come," so we cry out, "Come, Lord Jesus! Come! "

Today, out of the millions of Christians on the earth, there is only a relative handful crying out for the glory. I would venture to say, out of all the professing Christians, there is a large percent in the world today who are not crying out, "Lord, show me Thy glory." They are saying, "Lord, meet my needs and give me something practical that I can use on a daily basis."

I believe that there is nothing wrong with practical teaching because we must walk the walk on the earth. But where are the people who are saying, "Lord, Your glory is all we care about; Lord, manifest Yourself in the Church and manifest Yourself in our presence"?

I was never so shocked as I was a year ago when I was showing my close brethren videos of the manifestation of the glory that took place in North Carolina. There were only a handful, two or three out of the whole group who actually showed an interest. These are all men of God whom I count as my mentors and I respect them greatly. But there was almost a total indifference that they were witnessing such a manifestation.

Think about it! How could we ignore a move of God where God shows Himself and reveals Himself to us? How could we turn aside and have casual conversation when God is manifesting Himself in our midst? The Bible says in First Kings 8:11, "The priests could not continue ministering because of the cloud; for the glory of the Lord filled the house of the Lord." It was not simply because the glory knocked them down; it was because of their reverence as they beheld the glory of the Lord. They could not stand in His presence!

So this is the hour that we ought to count as precious and realize that we will either be changed by these manifestations or we will be repelled by them. You see, as the glory comes, it begins to separate those who have a hunger for God from those who do not, those who want the Kingdom of God from those who are building their own kingdom. If you have got your own kingdom to build, you do not want anything to interfere with your plans and programs.

Most churches today (and I am not trying to criticize churches), but most congregations today would not know how to accept the Lord's presence because if He came it would upset everything. We would say, "Well, there's His glory; now let me give this announcement real quick." Or, "Oh, His glory is here, but I've got to preach this message I prepared two weeks ago." Or, "His glory is here, but let's not delay getting out of church today because it might interfere with someone's dinner engagement."

Do we really want to make room for the glory? Do we really want Jesus to be so very prevalent in our midst, or would it interfere too much with our lifestyle?

Second Corinthians 3:7-8 says, "But if the ministry of death, written and engraved on stones, was glorious, so that the children of Israel could not look steadily at the face of Moses because of the glory of his countenance, which glory was passing away, how will the ministry of the Spirit not be more glorious?"

Paul is saying that what is going to happen in the new covenant is even more awesome than that which happened to Moses. His face so shone after encountering the Lord that people could not even look upon Him. Imagine what an incredible fear and awe fell on Israel when this occurred.

And the Lord says that in this hour, our hour, there is going to be something even greater. When Moses came down from the mountain his face was so radiant that he had to put a veil over it because the children of Israel could not receive it; they could not receive God's glory on Moses.

We do not want to be like those whom God has to conceal Himself from. We hunger for the Lord to come and give us the whole enchilada! We pray for the Lord to come and pour out more than we can contain. We want an abundance of anointing so that the overflow can splash out all around us and on to others.

It is not easy taking that position because you will be required to totally disregard what your natural mind is telling you. The natural mind hates depending on God because it interferes with our plans. But if we let our spirit rise up, we will be excited and cry out, "Bring me more, Lord, more of you, Lord!"

How can we deny this? How can we stay away from it? How can anyone miss even one church service if he or she knows there will be a manifestation of His glory? I will go and camp out there if I have to. What will you do just to be in a service like that?

In my heart I know I will do anything, sacrifice anything, give up anything to be there. What is more important—my agenda, or to have that revelation in my heart? Ask yourself, "What are the priorities of my life? Why am I in the church service and many are not?" It's not because you are more righteous than anyone else, but because your priorities are right. Be there because there might be a chance for you to have an encounter with God; there might be a manifestation of the Lord in the midst of the people. You see, whatever you set as your priority will be the outcome of your life.

Thirty years ago I set the house of the Lord as my priority and it remains my priority today. It does not make any difference how spiritual or unspiritual I am, how backslidden or unbacklidden I am. I make the house of the Lord my priority because I know my only hope is in the house of the Lord; my only hope is in the glory.

Many times, years have gone by in my life when I have not experienced God's manifested glory. You may have had the same thing happen to you. Yet, we continue to seek and cry out for more because we know that one day He will return again. I want to be ready when He comes; I want to be there when He manifests; I want His glory to be revealed in my midst. We welcome the Holy Spirit, not that we are sufficient of ourselves. As it says in Second

Corinthians 3:5, "Not that we are sufficient of ourselves to think of anything as being from ourselves, but our sufficiency is from God."

There are some people who are dull in their understanding and their perception, and they will never perceive His presence. God could come and manifest before them in great glory and they would say, "Huh! I didn't see or feel anything!" Or, "It's just some kind of visitation but I don't really know what's happening." It's because there is dullness in their heart. They have been lulled to sleep by the passivity of this age. That dullness in your heart can destroy you.

Others will say, "Behold the Lamb of God who takes away the sin of the world! Behold the Lord Jesus who cleanses me and restores my soul." To the same extent you open the door to your heart will the Lord restore your soul and reveal Himself to you—no more, no less. It is not God opening your heart; it is you opening your heart. God gives us the choice to determine our destiny by giving us our own will.

The choices you make determine the course you follow. If you make the wrong choices, you will find barrenness or unfruitfulness in your life. If you make the right choices, then He will lead you into the land of milk and honey. I do not believe it is an accident that one day we are here and the next day we are somewhere else. I believe everything is a matter of choice and what you choose determines the outcome of your life.

We choose obedience, to be led by the Spirit and not by the flesh. We choose for the Word of the Lord to be real to us, and to lead us, more than trusting in our own perceptions and opinions.

In Second Corinthians 4:6-8 Paul writes, "For it is the God who commanded light to shine out of darkness, who has shone in our hearts to give the light of the knowledge of the glory of God in the face of Jesus Christ. But we have this treasure in earthen vessels, that the excellence of the power may be of God and not of us. We are hard pressed on every side, yet not crushed; we are perplexed, but not in despair." Where is the Kingdom of God coming forth from in this hour? It is coming forth from you. You are the representatives of the Kingdom. As I look out at my congregation, I see a Kingdom before me. I do not just see a group of people; I see a mighty army of God.

I see mountain movers. I see prophets who will proclaim the Word of the Lord to the last generation. I see a house that will have more glory than the former house. I see that the ending of their lives will be greater than the beginning. Christians are the Kingdom; they are the called of the Lord, the chosen of God, the Holy Ones of Israel, the beloved of the Lord, the kingdom of priests unto our God. It is you!

Does that make you feel good? You can turn to the person seated beside you in your church and say, "You're the one!" And do not take that lightly, because your whole city, whole state, the entire nation, and all the earth could depend upon one little group of Christians. For it could be out of one small group that the whole earth is changed.

We do not say that from an arrogant or a presumptuous position; and when we do, we aren't discounting all the great servants of the Lord around the world, many far greater than us. We are saying, "Who knows the potential that's within us if we'll let the glory come?"

There was a prophecy given in 1973 in South Gate, California, a community in Los Angeles, and the prophecy said, "Out of Texas will come forth a mighty movement of the Holy Spirit that will evangelize the whole world." That prophecy came at the same exact moment that the Holy Spirit was being poured out in a church that we were at in Lubbock, Texas.

And so, do we look at our congregation and say, "Well, we're just a group small in number or a hidden band of people in a cave"? No! We are the Kingdom of God. Christ is within us, and He is the hope of glory for the whole earth. That means that within us is the power to change the whole world. So do not discount the days of small beginnings or despise that which other men would despise, but count it as joy, brethren, that you are a part of something that has such awesome potential.

We are involved in a company called KingsWay. We have thousands of people involved from around the country; and as I look at all those people, I know that one person out of the thousands, or even one who is yet to come, could revolutionize the world. One person could receive a revelation that will break through and cause mighty harvests like we have never seen before. It only takes one.

Look what one Billy Graham has done starting out as a farm boy from North Carolina. Look what one Michael Dell has done in less than a decade in the computer industry, going from zero, working out of a garage, to billions of dollars a year in sales. I am not comparing us to a business situation, but I am saying that there can be a release that comes to us that can cause a change to the whole earth.

We are not insignificant people who are here just passing the time and waiting for the day that we go six feet under or for the day when the Lord returns. We are a people destined to change the earth, "for this One has been counted worthy of more glory than Moses, inasmuch as He who built the house has more honor than the house" (Heb. 3:3).

In Matthew 16:19a, Jesus said, "And I will give you the keys of the kingdom of heaven." When someone gives you the keys, they are telling you that whatever is behind the door is yours. You can have it. I gave it to you; take advantage of it. In John chapter 17 we see this principle being laid out by the Lord; it is beautiful because He tells us that the same glory that He has, we can participate in. I like that about the Lord; He has no selfish ambition, no ego.

John 17:1 says, "Jesus spoke these words, lifted up His eyes to heaven, and said: 'Father, the hour has come. Glorify Your Son, that Your Son also may glorify You.' " That is the beautiful part about the glory. It is like a tape that keeps repeating, "glory and glory and glory, and glory." We are never to possess the glory and hide it for ourselves, but we are to continually share what we have received, which allows the glory to perpetually circulate.

That is why we do not ever keep money for ourselves. We are taught to continue circulating it in the Kingdom. The more you get, the more you ought to give. There is enough wealth in the world, that if distributed properly, no one should ever have to live in a substandard condition.

People say, "There's just not enough money in the world." That is not the case. There is plenty of money; there are just not enough givers. There are not enough kingdom-minded people. The enemy is a liar, and he has masked this truth to make it appear as though there is a shortage. But there isn't any lack; there is abundance. It is just a matter of distributing abundance to the people. There is so much wealth in God's Kingdom that every individual upon the earth could live like a king.

But even people who live in the greatest riches live substandard to His glory. Jesus tells us that all of the Father's riches are coming to us. In John chapter 17, He prays to the Father and speaks to the disciples in verse 5, "And now, O Father, glorify Me together with Yourself, with the glory which I had with You before the world was."

He wants to give us the glory. In verse 22, Jesus says, "And the glory which you gave Me I have given them, that they may be one just as We are one." When He says, "I have given," He is saying, "I gave, I am giving, and I will give." It is giving past, present, and future. He will continue to give this glory to His people.

The apostate church has robbed us of this victory. We have got to realize that it was only the beginning when the reformation came and Martin Luther said that we are justified and shall live by faith. Unfortunately, in the church world there is a deception that we have already arrived. But we will not reach our full potential until His glory returns to the earth. Stepping out in faith and believing in the Word is only the beginning. It is only the beginning to pray again and to worship again. Luke 1:33 tells us, "And He will reign over the house of Jacob forever, and of His kingdom there will be no end."

The Church has no end; it will give way to the glory. The Church is simply a mother who is birthing something greater than herself. There is a third dispensation. There is the old covenant, the new covenant, and the coming Kingdom. When we begin to walk in the Kingdom, we will look upon the Church just as the Church today looks upon the old covenant. God is in the process of birthing through us something greater than ourselves.

When we proclaim this message, it is often rejected, because most people's concept is that the Church is the final result. However, the Church is simply the vessel God has equipped and empowered to birth His earthly Kingdom.

When we walk in the Kingdom's principles, we are released into greater freedom than what we hold today. We can have glory upon us now if we are willing to put ourselves in a position where there is no turning back. Only the brave few who dare to live on the edge will be the ones who will break through to the greater glory. And once there is a breakthrough, many more will follow.

Jesus paid a price, and He had to do it all alone. We are able to see now how wonderful He was, although the people in His day did not recognize His worth. Most of them thought He was crazy, and only a handful of people stayed with Him. Even those who remained had a hard time doing so, and eventually forsook Him in His most crucial and difficult hours. But look what one man ushered in. The Bible says in Romans 5:12a, "Just as through one man [Adam] sin entered the world." But through this one man, Jesus, righteousness has come.

When Jesus went to the Mount of Transfiguration, He gave His disciples a glimpse of what was to come. Second Peter 1:16b says, "We were eyewitnesses of His majesty." And in Acts 1:9b, "While they watched, He [Jesus] was [*harpazo'd*] taken up, and a cloud received Him out of their sight." And I believe that was the cloud of glory. The unction came, the anointing came, and transformed Him into a transfigured state. Peter saw the transfigured Christ and what he saw is that which is to come.

When Christ appeared to them after His death, burial, and resurrection, they did not recognize Him in the natural. The state that Christ embodied is what we are approaching. The Church is transitioning out of a natural existence and into a spiritual one. As that starts to transpire, the two worlds will begin to merge closer together. That is why in our church we are beholding manifestations of the golden glory, the feathered glory, and the cloud glory. This transition from the natural to the spiritual is happening in different regions throughout the earth.

There is a merging of the Kingdom, and through these miraculous signs, God is saying to us that He is near. He wants you to enter into His presence through the veil. In many cases we act like it is a veil that still separates us from the mercy seat of God. Jesus was the veil who was rent in two and provided a passage to the heavenly presence of the Lord and into the abundance of His Kingdom.

What I am about to say could be used against me, but I decided a long time ago that I cannot let that stop me. There will be a people who will press into the third heaven, and they will be able to transfer what is in that realm into this one. In Matthew 6:10, Jesus said, "Your kingdom come. Your will be done on earth as it is in heaven."

There will be a people who will break through into the heavens, and they will begin to transfer power into the earthly realm. They will become the liberators of the earth. This power will liberate those who are bound by sin and death. Just as Jesus is the liberator, we are also liberators with Him, for we too are the anointed of God, the crystal of God, the chosen of God. Jesus said that He has chosen us to be glorified with Him. If He was caught up and glorified, what will we be doing? We are going to be caught up and become glorified also.

There will be one generation who breaks through into the glory realm, and they will become so radical that when it happens you will be astounded. If you are standing in the proper position, then God will use you and cause you to be a part of that generation of glory blazers. It is not because you are anything in and of yourself; it is because you will be at the right place, at the right time, doing the right thing, and you will break through.

In the last days there will be a famine in the land where people will be not only in a natural famine, but in a spiritual famine for hearing the Word. And suddenly, the fountain of living waters will spring forth and the anointing will be poured out. There will be a flowing of the Holy Spirit, accompanied by His Word, and men will say, "We've never heard such as this before; we've never dreamed possible that the Word could be so alive."

Men will have heard of the death of the Word, but all of a sudden the life of the Word will come. The shackles of the chains will begin to break and they will say, "Wow, I don't believe what we're hearing! This is the Word of life."

If you have never been in the light, you do not know what light is. You do not really know you are in darkness until the light turns on. Then all of a sudden the light comes on and boom! You say, "My goodness, what happened! What is this light? I've never seen light like this before! There is light, and then there is light, right? God is bringing a light that will break forth upon the earth. It will break down the barriers of the enemy. Out of this light the glory comes and is manifested in our midst.

Jesus said, "Hey Dad, this glory that You gave Me, I'm giving it to them so that they may be one with Us." Jesus is having a one-on-one conversation with the Father in John 17:23, "I in them, and You in Me; that they may be made perfect in one, and that the world may know that You have sent Me, and have loved them as You have loved Me."

The world is going to know that God loves you and not just because you go around saying, "God loves me." They will know because of the noticeable separation in your life from that which is worldly. His blessing and glory will be so evident upon your life that there will be no denying it.

The world has become increasingly cynical. In America, cynicism and agnosticism is at an all-time high. We have an entire generation of people who have not been raised in church tradition or any other forms of man-made doctrine. I believe because of their openness God is able to prepare them for the glory. I have discovered that those people who have been ingrained in doctrine and tradition are finding it harder to receive the supernatural glory than those people who have not had the same background. Sometimes those who are pure agnostics or atheists are more apt to receive God and His glory than the religious people.

It is the stiff-necked people who see something that is supernatural and say, "This can't be from God; it must be of the devil." But the agnostics look at it and say, "Wow, this must be something special to be manifesting like this!"

Jesus said in John 17:24a, "Father, I desire that they also whom You gave Me may be with Me where I am, that they may behold My glory." When you look to find Jesus, do not pray to pictures and statues or say He is in your heart. Jesus is found seated at the right hand of the Father. So where should we behold Him? We should behold Him at the Father's side.

We begin learning to behold Jesus by looking with the eyes of faith. Some of you might have seen Him with your natural eyes under certain circumstances and at a certain time, but by and large, most of us have not. However, we can learn to fix our focus completely on Him and gaze intently into His face with our spiritual eyes.

If you are mature in Christ, you can discipline yourself to behold the Lord anytime you decide. We can look at Jesus, seated at the right hand of the Father, full of glory. The Bible says in Second Corinthians 3:18, "But we all, with unveiled face, beholding as in a mirror the glory of the Lord, are being transformed into the same image from glory to glory, just as by the Spirit of the Lord."

Your ability to see God's glory will set the pace of your transformation. In most cases the process is very slow. The flesh is incapable of absorbing such a radical change all at once. Your natural brain would fry if you did not have a transitional period.

A good analogy is the metamorphosis that turns a caterpillar into a butterfly. This transition is not something that takes place in a day; it's a process. But if we get ourselves in the proper place and keep the proper focus, the transformation can take place until the finished result is a beautiful butterfly. We start out as worms, but our goal is to fly, to become a butterfly set free for Jesus. Where the Spirit of the Lord is, there is liberty.

Jesus said in John 17:25-26, "O righteous Father! The world has not known You, but I have known You; and these have known that You sent Me. And I have declared to them Your name, and will declare it, that the love with which You loved Me may be in them, and I in them."

When we behold the Lord and follow His example, we are changed into His image and become like Him. The same love and generosity that God has will begin to flow out of us. The same compassion will begin to grab our hearts, the same concern for humanity, and the same desire to bring others into His glory.

He will reward those who diligently seek Him, so seek Him and let your heart be lifted up to a higher realm that you might know Him in the power of His resurrection and be transformed by His presence.

CHAPTER 3

I See the Holy Place

The Lord desires to lift us up from the place of blind faith to a place where we see the supernatural manifesting in our midst. When we have a unique spiritual experience, when the anointing comes, or when revelation from God is released in our heart, it is a confirmation of that which God has already spoken to us.

The Bible says in the last days we will go from glory to glory and from image to image. In other words, there will be greater experiences than we have previously known. We do not live by experiences, we walk by faith; but experience is inevitable because it is God's way of confirming what He has spoken.

In our church there have been consistent manifestations taking place that are evidence of the times in which we live. The Bible says that we can always judge the times by the seasons. It is obvious to us when it is winter time. It is obvious when it is spring or summer or fall, and so it is in the Spirit. It is obvious when there is a particular anointing in our midst or when God is moving in a special way.

The Feast of Tabernacles was one of the seven sacred feasts the children of Israel would observe, marking the transition from the old to the new. The people would come to Jerusalem and gather together at the feast of foods. They would commemorate the time when the nation of Israel was wandering in the wilderness. The men would stand in their tents and observe the cloud of glory as it descended on a place called the tent of meeting.

There is only one of two places you can be. Either you are looking at the tabernacle from a distance or you are inside. To be inside the tent of meeting means that you will experience what God is bringing firsthand, not just hear about it as the Israelites did through Moses. I believe all of us want to be in the tent and need to hear God speak to us personally.

It is like going to church and listening to a preacher talk about the things of God, yet never experiencing the wonders for yourself. But God's intention is to bring us all into the secret place where He is talking to us face to face.

Interestingly Hebrews 8:11a says, "None of them shall teach his neighbor, and none his brother, saying, 'Know the Lord.'" Why? Because in verse 10, the Lord says, "I will put My laws in their mind and write them on their hearts." That is the highest level we could possibly achieve. Jesus lived in a realm that was so fantastic because He walked in a divine state of always hearing what the Father was saying and seeing what the Father was doing.

I often say that you can only become as great as what you see yourself becoming. Or, you can only do the things that you see yourself doing. In the world, motivational speakers teach the same principles. They teach that what you see is what you get. It is the same principal for our spiritual walk as well, because what we believe for is what becomes our reality. The problem for many people is that they are expecting to receive without ever having believed.

To believe something is not simply the mental consent to say "I believe because someone told me about it." To have true faith demands action in the sense that it requires you to grasp what is set before you. The Bible says in Hebrews 12:1b-2, "Let us lay aside every weight, and the sin which so easily ensnares us, and let us run with endurance the race that is set before us, looking unto Jesus, the author and finisher of our faith, who for the joy that was set before Him endured the cross, despising the shame, and has sat down at the right hand of the throne of God."

Hebrews 10:23 (KJV) says, "Let us hold fast the profession of our faith...." Once we grab faith, it will then become our experience.

If we are just beholding it from a distance, it is not our experience; it is someone else's.

In the wilderness, Moses, Joshua, and Caleb were continually filled with the Spirit. When crunch time came, as it comes to all of us, it was only Joshua and Caleb who were able to enter into the promised land. (God had another plan for Moses.) Joshua and Caleb were the only two who had remained in the presence of the Lord long enough to instill in their spirits the boldness and confidence they needed to inherit the promised land. The original generation of Israelites who were led out of Egypt perished in the wilderness.

If we want to be victorious in our life, then we must come to the place that we not only visualize our destiny but we believe in our dreams until they are fulfilled. We do not hold back, but we press in until it becomes our reality. In Philippians 3:13-14, Paul writes, "Brethren, I do not count myself to have apprehended; but one thing I do, forgetting those things which are behind and reaching forward to those things which are ahead, I press toward the goal for the prize of the upward call of God in Christ Jesus." There is a labor that takes place to birth us into the next level, and it often requires all the strength that is within us to get there.

Nothing of enduring value comes easy. It's easy street once you break through, but before that, it is like a woman in labor during childbirth. There is a painful time; but once the head crowns, once the baby is born, then the victory is there and the whole experience changes. The pain may linger, but our focus is not on the pain; it's on the joy.

Hebrews 8:1-2 says, "Now this is the main point of the things we are saying: We have such a High Priest, who is seated at the right hand of the throne of the Majesty in the heavens, a Minister of the sanctuary and of the true tabernacle which the Lord erected, and not man."

So let's visualize this for just a minute. The Lord Jesus Christ is in Heaven, seated at the right hand of the Father. He is on the throne as our minister and priest over a sanctuary and a tabernacle erected by His own hands. This is a brand-new dimension of the atonement than what we have seen in the old covenant. Instead of man offering sacrifices to cover his sins, the Lord Jesus Christ is the sacrificial offering on our behalf through the cross. What I want you to focus on is what the writer of Hebrews is saying. There is a place in the Spirit that Christ can be found.

The Scripture goes on to contrast how there is a tabernacle on earth that has been built by the hands of men. The priests have created a copy, a shadow of the heavenly things. Everything that is in the heavenly tabernacle is mimicked in the earthly realm.

Why is it important that we practice certain demonstrative patterns in our worship service to God? It is because we are attempting to mimic that which is taking place in Heaven. Some people ask, "Does it make any difference how you worship?" Well, it makes all the difference in the world, because until you can link up to how worship is in Heaven, how prayer is in Heaven, and how ministry is taking place in Heaven, you will merely portray a form of godliness, but lack the power thereof. But, we should be careful to never lock ourselves into a pattern; we should always remain open to change when God leads us into a different direction.

When I was caught up in the throne room of God in 1989, what was most impressive was the worship that was taking place. Everything that was there existed for one reason only, and that was to worship the Lord. It was an awesome experience! I saw people in the throne room who looked like us, but there were other creatures there as well, including the cherubim, all worshiping the Lord and all gathered around the throne of God.

A continual expression of worship inhabits Heaven, and it is in that atmosphere where true freedom can be found. It is only through the expression of worship that we have the ability to cease functioning in the natural and become able to ascend to a higher spiritual plane. Only when we are able to suppress the natural and press into the spiritual will we ever have any life-changing encounters with God.

In John 4:23, Jesus says, "But the hour is coming, and now is, when the true worshipers will worship the Father in spirit and truth; for the Father is seeking such to worship Him." Until we learn to abide in the Spirit we cannot become true worshipers. We can be pretenders to the throne; but we do not want to be pretenders, for we have been called to be the true sons of God.

Jesus made it possible for all of us to come before God's throne. Before Jesus came, men had to depend upon a priest for access to God. Some people still believe that you must have an advocate with the Father in the form of a priest on earth. But now we know an Advocate who is not an earthly priest, but a heavenly one.

When Jesus died on the cross, the veil that held man back from knowing God personally was rent from top to bottom. Because of this, we now have the ability to go beyond the veil into the Holy of Holies where the Lord is.

Hebrews 8:4-5a says, "For if He were on earth, He would not be a priest, since there are priests who offer the gifts according to the law; who serve the copy and shadow of the heavenly things...." What were the priests on earth serving? They were serving the copy and the shadow of heavenly things. The earthly tabernacle, built by man, was a copy and a shadow of that which is heavenly or divine.

In the Old Testament, we see how the Lord instructed them to build a tabernacle. Hebrews 9:1 talks about the tabernacle. "Then indeed, even the first covenant had ordinances of divine service and the earthly sanctuary." When we look at the copy, the earthly tabernacle, we can get a glimpse of how the spiritual tabernacle operates and how it applies to our life.

The old covenant has been fulfilled, but that does not mean we should disregard its former purposes. In my house there are a lot of obsolete things that I've never done away with; I probably should throw them out. But we should not throw out the old laws and traditions in the Word of God, because each time we study the imagery and symbolism of the old covenant, it portrays the new covenant and reminds us of spiritual laws we are to pattern ourselves by.

It is unfortunate when someone tries to accept the new covenant, this new relationship that God has given us through Jesus, and the truth into their heart, but then returns to the obsolete things and drags them out of the closet. Those old things will only create death. They represent the spirit of religion, an age-old problem.

Some people tend to cling to man-made traditions they were raised with. They want what is familiar to stay with them. It is all right to honor your past, but you have to look at it in the proper perspective. You must never count on tradition to give you the ability to maintain a continual relationship with the Lord. Tradition will always pull you back into its confinement, and it will never bring liberty. It is only when you break away from the old that you can experience the new.

As long as your mind is set upon that which was, you will never experience that which is to be. We know that to be true in success principles, but it is even truer in spiritual principles. We can never walk in the new covenant as long as we believe the old covenant is what brings us life. Our life consists of only what Christ has done for us; there is not an earthly tabernacle that has ever been built that will be able to supply you with one ounce of life. No earthly traditions or the doctrines of men, or even traditions of the old covenant will bring you righteousness. But they will point you to where the life is, if you will look at them in the proper perspective.

Do not disdain that which you came out of; you are to honor it like a child would honor his parents. But when the child grows up and starts to live his own adult life with his own family, he doesn't continue to hold on to his parents. The parents were simply a launching pad to go to the next level.

When we look at the covenant in the sanctuary, we see how the Lord directs us, and keeps ever pointing us to the spiritual, because our goal is to be at the throne. I want to have instant access into His presence.

I close my eyes and instantly I am able to go to the throne. You don't have to close your eyes; I do it simply to help me get in the Spirit. The Spirit does not get in you; you've got to get in Him. On Sunday morning before I preach, when I am standing before the people and praising the Lord, I'll start drinking out of a cup. Now probably some people in the church think there is wine in the cup, but actually the cup is empty! But I keep drinking by faith, and the more I drink it, the more drunk I become, because I am drinking in the Spirit. I am doing it by faith.

The faith that I have, or that you have, could instantly transform us from natural to spiritual; and the more we exercise our faith, the faster we can have access. It is called practicing the presence of the Lord. I don't walk around every day, every moment, every hour saying, "Ohhh, I'm in the Spirit." But I can get there real quick. I live and have to function in a natural world, but I always have one eye tuned to the spiritual world because that is where my life source is coming from.

Hebrews chapter 9 tells us that in the tabernacle there were three primary courts: the outer court, the inner court, (which was called the Holy Place), and the Holy of Holies. Each court represents a different level of relationship that we can obtain with the Lord. The outer court represents the entryway, or the place that most people live. They are in the place in which they are aware something is close by, yet they do not know quite how to obtain it. That is living in frustration, isn't it? One way I define frustration is to be denied access.

I get very frustrated if I try to open a door and find it locked. When I was younger and had a hothead temper (which I don't have anymore, thank You, Jesus), and I came to a locked door, I would just kick it in. I would rather kick in the door and pay for the damages than be frustrated by not being able to enter into the room. The Lord delivered me from that, and besides, I got tired of my feet hurting.

The outer court is a place where people are frustrated because they are struggling to find an answer. Most of us go through this more often than not, struggling to find answers. We struggle to find peace, struggle to find joy or fulfillment in our lives. It is an outer court experience. It is a place of futility, a place where we know there is a promise, we know that there is a call, we know there is a hope; but yet we do not quite know how to get to the next level. That is the outer court.

There are people that do go on to the next level, and the Bible calls this place the Holy Place. In the Holy Place was found the table of shewbread, the golden lampstand, and the altar of incense. In the old covenant the Holy Place was the court that only the priests could enter into. Of course, in the new covenant you also have access, because the Bible calls you a royal priesthood. The primary function of a priest is to find his position before God. Then he has God's attentive ear and is able to commune with God.

Out of the primary function, communing with God, the priest can perform his secondary call, which is to convey what God is speaking to the people and also convey God's forgiveness to the people. The priest would carry the sins of the people upon his shoulders, giving them absolution and forgiveness.

What did Jesus Christ do? He took our sins and carried them on the cross so that we could be forgiven, because sins could only be forgiven through a living sacrifice. In the old covenant the sacrifice was an animal. The people would shed the blood of an animal, for without the shedding of blood, the Scripture tells us, there is no remission of sin. Until one life is given, another life cannot be redeemed.

Now in the Holy Place the priest would enter and purify himself, preparing himself for the next level. Most people are satisfied if they can just get to the Holy Place. But really, the Holy Place is simply a preparation for a higher place. In the tabernacle it was called the Holy of Holies. This was the third step, and in the Bible, three represents perfection.

Many people believe that there are three levels to Heaven because Paul said he was caught up to the third heaven. I not only believe that, but I'm convinced that once this earthly life is over, you will have the ability to reach the highest level. But there will be many who will remain in the outer court.

Will there be frustration and futility in Heaven? Not the way we know futility here, but those who have not walked closely with the Lord here will not have the opportunity to walk with Him on the intimate level that is so awesome there. They will see Jesus. They will behold Him, they will feel His presence, they will observe His ways; but they will not have intimate communion with Him.

We want in this life to be so closely tied in with the Lord so that we are not mere acquaintances from a distance, but we are personal friends. In John 15:15b, Jesus said, "I have called you friends, for all things that I heard from My Father I have made known to you." And that is our desire—to be called His friends.

How many know that there are friends, and then there are friends? You can develop such a close relationship with someone, but it is rare to have more than one person in your entire life that you have that level of friendship with. You know that no matter what you confide to that person, no matter what you confess, no matter what you expose of yourself, that person will cover your backside and stand alongside you. That is true friendship, isn't it?

There are other people whom you have a guarded friendship with because if you expose yourself and all your faults to them, their tendency will be to not have the same faith in you as they had before. But a true friend will love in all seasons. A true friend is born in adversity. A true friend never gives up on you. A true friend always forgives. They might correct you and even chastise you some, but they will forgive you because they have made a covenant with you.

Well, this is the relationship that the Lord wants to have with you. His covenant with us is so endearing that He wants our relationship with Him to be likened to the same that He had with Peter, James, and John. Jesus had 12 disciples, but only three went with Him to the Mount of Transfiguration. They were the only ones who beheld Him when He was transformed supernaturally by the Father's glory. We know all the other disciples loved Jesus too. They walked with Him and followed Him, yet only three held a close, intimate relationship with the Lord. There's the number three again.

The Lord loved John so much that John 13:23 says, "Now there was leaning on Jesus' bosom one of His disciples, whom Jesus loved." John was so close to the Lord that Jesus did not become embarrassed nor did He push His beloved friend away. While the disciple reclined his head against the Lord's chest, Jesus continued speaking to all of the disciples in the upper room.

In the tabernacle, beyond the Holy Place, beyond the veil, is the Holy of Holies or "Holiest of all." Hebrews 9:3-4 says, "And behind the second veil, the part of the tabernacle which is called the Holiest of All, which had the golden censer and the ark of the covenant overlaid on all sides with gold, in which were the golden pot that had the manna, Aaron's rod that budded, and the tablets of the covenant."

Hebrews tells us that in the Most Holy Place, the ark of the covenant was overlaid on all sides with gold, in which was the golden pot that had the manna, Aaron's rod that budded, and the tablets of the covenant. Above it were the cherubim of glory overshadowing the mercy seat. Now because everything in the old tabernacle is a type and a shadow, we could say our churches are also a type and a shadow. As the day of the Kingdom gets closer, we will be unmistakably identified with the Word of the Lord, and all that God has spoken will become a reality for us.

In our church we have been witnessing manifestations of gold. People have asked, "What's the purpose of the gold?" The purpose is not to have it analyzed to see if it is the gold that man knows, or to try and sell it, or to exalt someone who has it. Gold represents an intricate part of intimacy. A man gives his new bride a ring of gold to wear to symbolize their covenant together. So too, our heavenly Bridegroom is symbolizing His intimacy with us. The Lord is saying, "You are getting closer and closer to My Holy Place. You are getting closer to the place where I am going to abide with you." Psalm 68:13 says, "Though you lie down among the sheepfolds, you will be like the wings of a dove covered with silver, and her feathers with yellow gold."

We are also witnessing a supernatural manifestation that we call "the feather glory." During our prayer meetings, we are honored to have a cloud of feathers hover above us as we worship the Lord. I believe it is symbolic of the Lord's train, the Lord's presence in our midst. Isaiah 6:1 says, "In the year that King Uzziah died, I saw the Lord sitting on a throne, high and lifted up, and the train of His robe filled the temple."

The great challenge and the question that the Church faces in this hour is: Do we really believe in the supernatural moves of God? Many profess to believe, but when the Lord begins to move in miraculous ways, there are those in the Body who are quick to try and discredit the "new." Often the unbelievers will receive a new move of God, while the formal church as a whole might reject it.

Jesus told us that it would not be the self-righteous ones who receive Him, but in the last days the greatest salvation will come to the prostitute, the tax collector, the heathen, and the people who are unbelievers. Those are the ones who will be wowed by the presence of the Lord even more so than the church.

There will always be a remnant of the church that will surface. When the glory begins to be revealed, there will be a coming out, an exodus that will take place. And then people will begin to stream to the house of the Lord. They will come to behold the glory of the Lord.

> *Now when these things had been thus prepared, the priests always went into the first part of the tabernacle, performing the services. But into the second part the high priest went alone once a year, not without blood, which he offered for himself and for the people's sins committed in ignorance; the Holy Spirit indicating this, that the way into the Holiest of All was not yet made manifest while the first tabernacle was still standing. It was symbolic for the present time in which both gifts and sacrifices are offered which cannot make him who performed the service perfect in regard to the conscience—concerned only with foods and drinks, various washings, and fleshly ordinances imposed until the time of reformation. But Christ came as High Priest of the good things to come, with the greater and more perfect tabernacle not made with hands, that is, not of this creation* (Hebrews 9:6-11).

So Christ has come now to usher us into the holiest place of all. His Spirit is saying to our hearts that He has committed Himself to us and that He came and gave everything on our behalf. Because of that commitment, we too should be compelled to commit in return.

The only response to commitment is that you try to bring a matched response, thus establishing an equal relationship. It is hard to have a relationship with someone if you are the only one who is committing yourself. How many wives or how many husbands have had this problem? They say, "Well, my wife (or husband) won't work on the problem." If you are the only one who is working on it, the relationship is not going to work.

The Lord has committed all of Himself to us, so for us to prove our true devotion, we must aim to meet Him at His level. It will take a lifetime to try to match His commitment because His is the perfect example. But the level of commitment that we rise to will be the level of communion that we will enjoy with Him.

When someone says, "How long should I believe God before I become discouraged?" Well, the moment you ask that question you are telling me that you will never find fulfillment because your commitment will be tested over and over again.

Does a young person considering marriage ask, "How long should I stay in this marriage? I'm getting married to someone, but should I stay in it for two years, or five, or ten, or twenty years, or thirty years? Should I set a time limit on this marriage?" No, when you step into a marriage, it's forever. Now God grants divorce according to the hardness of people's hearts, but God's intention is for that marriage to last forever.

"Well, how long should I believe God?" Forever. "How long should I hold on to the promise?" Forever. "You mean, even if I don't see the fulfillment of it, I keep believing?" Yes, because God is not a liar. "For whatever a man sows, that he will also reap" (Gal. 6:7). Don't be deceived, don't mock God; His promises are sure and true.

So even if we do not see promises fulfilled, we still commit. That is the greatest test of faith. To commit to something without any evidence of completion is the highest level of faith. When you find someone like that, they cannot be stopped. When someone is determined to reach that level, there is no way they can ever be defeated.

Many years ago I made commitments to the Lord, and if you were to ask me, "Do you feel like all that you have committed has brought the kind of fruit that you wanted?" the overwhelming majority of the time I would have to say no.

Through the difficult challenges that I have faced pastoring churches, there have been those who have challenged my manhood and authority. I have had some tell me that I am a failure and do not deserve to be a pastor. Throughout the years, the accusers have hurled their disapproving words at me, and it has hurt my feelings.

But if you listen and believe those types of reports, you will never hit the mark because it is the enemy speaking to you. The enemy will come to you and say, "Well, look at you. You've got this fault, and that fault. You're so inadequate. You lack this and that, and you don't deserve anything from God." The enemy's job is to try and wear down the saints of the Most High, to convince you that you are a loser and that you would be better off dead. He comes to steal, kill, and destroy.

The way you overcome is to make your commitment and your covenant so final that there are no options, no turning back. Why am I still here after over 30 years of walking with God? Why am I still preaching?

It is not because I haven't had opportunities in life to pursue other options. I am still preaching because I made a commitment to the Lord. I have not always wanted to preach, or always felt like preaching, but I continue on because of my commitment.

I'm not trying to put a halo around my head and tell you I'm a saint. But every time I waver and every time I want to quit, I go back to the day that I drove a stake in the ground in Louisiana and said, "Lord, don't ever let me turn back from what You've called me to do. If I ever do, take me out of here." It was a life or death commitment. I am committed for life.

I am shoring up that commitment even more in my life today, and I am encouraging you to do the same. Let your commitment level rise up to the point that when the enemy comes, when the storms, waves, and afflictions come (and they will), you will not back away. You will say, "I believe God; I believe God; I believe God for the fulfillment of His promises in my generation, my church, my home, and in my personal life. I believe the Lord, amen."

Above every report of the enemy, believe God in your commitment level. The Lord may tarry and succeeding generations may come after us. The lasting testament we want to leave with our children and our grandchildren is for them to look back upon our generation, upon our lives and say, "My grandfather and my grandmother, or that sister or brother whom I knew, they were rock solid. They were committed to the Lord and to the promise above everything else." That becomes the strength by which they can draw inspiration.

I had that strength in my grandmother. She was the primary one who became my anchor, or my foundation, through which I built and based my whole relationship with God. It is as though I stepped up on her back and reached the next level because she was committed. She never had much, lived in a little old house, and had to endure an abusive husband for years. She raised a family in the sand hills around Muleshoe, Texas, starting off in an adobe mud shack and after that, moving to a little wood plank shack. In her later years she lived in a modest frame house only two blocks from the Methodist church that she loved so much.

She had osteoporosis and was bent over, earning her living ironing other people's clothes. She worked at that job until she passed away in her eighties, but during my grandmother's whole life she was so committed to the Lord that she left a legacy for me. Her one life that seemed so insignificant to many was the most significant life to me. No matter what you think about your position in life, you can be a great example to others through your commitment, your faithfulness, and your desire to be in the Holy Place.

We are breaking through, not just for ourselves; we are breaking through for the generations among us. We are pressing into this glory, not just so that we can get holy goose bumps and get drunk on the wine of the Kingdom, we are pressing in for this glory so that the glory of God can be seen all over the earth.

It's like a big dam, and if we put a hole in it, the water will start spewing out. What we have is contagious; it is glorious, it is awesome. And as we manifest God's glory, it creates a hunger in people for more of the presence of the Lord. To God be the glory; great things He has done, for He is mighty and He is awesome in our midst. He alone is worthy to be praised, and we give Him the glory and honor and praise.

Chapter 4

The Mercy Seat

The Lord is speaking to my heart that the only significant thing that matters at this point is that we press in to know Him and His presence. We know that doctrine will not change us and tradition will not change us; only the presence of the Lord changes us. To be in His presence for one moment is far greater than reading all the books that have ever been written and hearing all the tales that have ever been told. Everything that has ever happened in history pales in comparison to one glimpse of the glory of the Lord.

Every significant event that has taken place in my life has been as a result of an encounter with God: close encounters of the God kind. Second Corinthians 3:18 tells us that we are going to experience a glory, and then another glory, and then another. What is glory? Glory is the presence of God evidenced and manifested in our midst. Glory is something that is actually tangible.

The great manifestation of the glory cloud began coming to our church during a Friday night prayer meeting. Glory came at the precise moment that I spoke these words, "The Lord had shown me that the altar here represents the mercy seat which will be overshadowed with the cloud of the Lord, as it is written in Hebrews 9:5." A cloud literally appeared over our heads and we were all instantly aware, very much so, of His presence and of the glory of the Lord.

The glory that was manifested in the Old Testament was called the *shekinah*—the brightness and splendor emanating from God in the pillar of cloud and in the Holy of Holies. When His divinity appeared in a cloud in the sanctuary where the people were assembled, the priests could not remain standing to minister. Their physical bodies were not able to stand in the awesome presence of the Lord. We understand that in our church. Once while trying to minister, I found it difficult to remain standing and kept falling backwards. The more His presence came, the harder it was to stand.

We live in a time when the formal church has basically been skeptical and unbelieving. To claim to be a Christian and to actually experience Christ are two different things. In the world there is a great population that carries the name Christian, but there is only a remnant out of that vast number who have actually experienced Christ, who have actually had Jesus come into their hearts and have been born again. Jesus said in John 3:3, "Most assuredly, I say to you, unless one is born again, he cannot see the kingdom of God."

Today the Lord wants you to experience Him like the woman did in Luke chapter 8. She was stricken with an infirmity for 12 agonizing years, but with faith and persistence she reached out and touched the hem of Jesus' garment. The Lord's response was, "I perceived power going out from Me" (v. 46b). Transference will take place because the minute you touch the Lord, He will transfer His power to meet all your needs. His blood will cleanse you from your sin and shame. Jesus will exchange all our death, fear, and sorrow for His life, His peace, and His joy.

The Lord wants to give you far more than you are capable of ever giving Him. The Scriptures tell us that Christ first loves us. I like that. He initiates His love towards us. Even in our backslidden, hardened, passive condition, He continues to express how much He loves us. That's incredible.

The Book of Hosea talks about Hosea's wife and how he continued loving her even though she was a harlot. Because of this type of unconditional love, Christ can win us. No matter how corrupt our hearts are, or how estranged we are from God, His love is so consistent that He can still win us over. I have wrestled with God probably more often than most people have. I have struggled throughout my life to keep from doing what God wanted me to do. Now that might come as a surprise to you, but that is my nature.

A prophecy came to me in the '70s that I was like Jacob. Before he wrestled with the Lord, Jacob was a deceiver, a liar, and a strong-willed person. But after wrestling with the Lord, after a great struggle with God, he became Israel, the prince of the Lord. He experienced a total transformation of character that took place through his encounter with God.

And that is what takes place in my life, and I know in yours, each time we encounter the living Christ. Our character is transformed and our nature is changed into His image.

Younger people tend to be very goal oriented. They are highly competitive in their games and are continually looking towards the future; there is always a goal in mind in everything they do. What should be the goal of a Christian? The primary goal of the Christian is to become like Him, to be like Jesus.

One time a man in our church told me that his child was going to bless me. The child said to his parent, "That's not the pastor, that's Jesus." Well I appreciated the compliment. I'm obviously not Jesus, but it was honoring to hear that I represented the nature of Christ to the child. Of course, we who are older know how far from the truth that really is. But that is God's plan—He wants Jesus to be revealed in you.

Christ in you becomes the hope of the whole earth. Romans 8:22 says it: "For we know that the whole creation groans and labors with birth pangs together until now." Why is the earth in such travail? Romans 8:19 says, "For the earnest expectation of the creation eagerly waits for the revealing of the sons of God." How do we become manifested to the world as a son of God? It happens by the nature of Christ being formed in us. We are being changed from glory to glory, and from image to image.

Hebrews 8 and 9 talks about the transition of covenant from the old to the new that took place through Jesus. He is the mediator of the new covenant. It is by Him and through Him that we are able to transcend out of the old covenant into the new that God has prepared for us. The new covenant promises mercy and grace, and a bond of intimacy. The old covenant has been fulfilled, yet it represents and reveals to us what the new covenant encompasses.

Hebrews chapter 8 illustrates the tabernacle as a type, a symbol, and a shadow of what is to come. We want to look at the relevancy of the Word today and how the tabernacle is a revelation of the Kingdom.

A kingdom exists only when there is a king and a people for the king to reign over. A king without any subjects is a king without a kingdom. It is like being part of a royal family but having a title in name only. It means nothing. Your name may be "Sir" this or "Madam" that, but it really means nothing if you are not sir-ing or madam-ing over anyone.

A true kingdom is one with people. We are in God's Kingdom, and we are under a King. Because of Christ we have been elevated to a new stature. We have been brought out of the depraved condition of humanity, and we have married into royalty. Because we serve Him and love Him, we are becoming one with Him and taking on His very nature.

The King, the Lord Jesus Christ who rules, is establishing a Kingdom of people who have the same heart that He has, the same motivation and the same love and compassion. We are becoming that people. The key is to get to the place where you have fully enacted the covenant into your life—in other words, where Jesus Christ is really your Lord.

Now we all start out in Christ at the point of salvation. To become saved gives us entry into a certain portion of the Kingdom. As I mentioned before, Hebrews 9 describes the tabernacle and the three divisions in the tabernacle—the outer court, an inner court (the Holy Place), and a final court called the Holy of Holies.

The outer court is the place where we all bear witness of Christ because it is there that we first enter into the presence of the Lord. In this court there is a faint presence of the glory. The people who remain in this court live for God just close enough to where they feel their conscience can be eased.

The outer court person comes to church occasionally so he or she can get a small dose of God. They are not really pressing in. During the week their lives are chaotic and frustrating, and they live in futility because there is no fruit of the Spirit. They are tossed to and fro. If there is an announcement of disasters or economic problems on the news, they cower in fear, just like the world does. They are outer court people.

If something happens in their personal lives, they panic. Because they are living in the outer court, they do not have the resources of the inner court. They do not have the strength and the life that comes from the inside court called the Holy Place. It is in the outer court that we become susceptible to destruction, because we do not have the covering of the Lord.

The apostle Paul said he was caught up to the third heaven and he saw things that he could not even speak about. Since there is mention of a third heaven, there must be other heavens as well. There are degrees of inheritance and degrees of appropriation that take place in the Kingdom. I believe, when some die and are resurrected, they will be in the outer court of His presence. They will be able to see Him from a distance and behold His glory from a distance. They will have a certain amount of fellowship simply by association, but they will not have the same level of intimacy as those who have pressed in to the holiest place.

As I mentioned before, Jesus and His disciples evidence these levels of intimacy. There were 12 disciples, but how many did He take to the Mount of Transfiguration? He took only three: Peter,

James, and John. Now, why were they singled out to go to the mount, to behold the most glorious demonstration of the presence of God that had ever been witnessed by man in the history of humanity?

Only three were chosen because of their relationship to the Lord. They had pressed in to be more than just followers; they had committed to become a brother and a friend to the Lord. He said that the highest honor was that now He could call them His friends. Now He could call those whom He had joined Himself to, His Bride. He had made covenant with them.

And so we have a choice to make, don't we? We can be outer court Christians who love the Lord, but who are not willing to become sanctified and separated from the spirit of the world. We can choose to keep ourselves at a distance because we are afraid that if we go any further it will require more washing to take place in our life.

You see, the further you go into His presence, the more you must be willing to let the Lord examine and circumcise your heart. David was a man after God's own heart, and he said in Psalm 26:2, "Examine me, O Lord, and prove me; try my mind and my heart."

The further we go in the spirit, in the presence of the Lord, the greater the dealings of God we will face. The greater the relationship you develop with Him, the greater the commitment and sanctification He will require of you. Without holiness no man can see the Lord. We know that not one of us are holy in the sense that our flesh is righteous enough that we deserve any merit before God. But it is not the flesh that He is speaking about. It is the heart that says, "Lord, I want to know You above everything else."

Paul had this kind of heart for God. He said in Philippians 3:10: "That I may know Him and the power of His resurrection, and the fellowship of His sufferings, being conformed to His death."

Why are manifestations taking place in our church? It is not because somehow, some way, God just popped in by accident one day. It is because there are people in the church who have wholly followed and sought after the presence of the Lord. It is not something that occurs because we just happen to be here, but as it says in Hebrews 11:6b, "He is a rewarder of those who diligently seek Him."

You can live in the outer court and never really seek the Lord. You can watch the priests coming and going, and as they pass by, you can cry out, "Oh, please say a prayer for me; please tell Him to forgive my sins. Oh, tell Him I need money; tell Him I need a relationship; tell Him I need something, please!" Outer court people never know how to come boldly to the throne of grace for their own needs. They are always dependent upon someone else to fulfill their needs and not on the Lord Himself.

Inner court people appreciate other people praying for them and helping them out, but by and large they take it upon themselves to press in to the presence of God. We would put Christian counselors out of business if everybody were inner court people. The only reason we need counseling is because without clear communication from the Lord we do not have direction. The closer you get to the Lord the more you will hear His voice speaking directly to you and the less confusion you will have in your life.

Confusion comes from lack of communication. Why do you think the devil tries so hard to keep you from hearing God's voice? His strategy is to confuse you so he can keep you defeated. The outer court is not the place we want to be. In the outer court you are not able to maintain a continual sense of forgiveness. The moment you feel condemnation, or that you are not forgiven, is the very moment you shut yourself off from the Lord.

Inner court people walk in a sense of forgiveness, not only being forgiven, but forgiving others as well. They cannot hold in their heart bitterness and resentment against anyone. Outer court people find forgiving a struggle because they let themselves become bitter. They have remained too far off in the distance to allow the Lord to minister to them up close and personal. Without the Lord's anointing, it is very difficult for outer court people to minister or help anyone.

The inner court is a much better place. It is called the Holy Place. In Hebrews 9:2-5 we read,

> *For a tabernacle was prepared: the first part, in which was the lampstand, the table, and the show-bread, which is called the sanctuary; and behind the second veil, the part of the tabernacle which is called the Holiest of All, which had the golden censer and the ark of the covenant overlaid on all sides with gold, in which were the golden pot that had the manna, Aaron's rod that budded, and the tablets of the covenant; and above it were the cherubim of glory overshadowing the mercy seat. Of these things we cannot now speak in detail.*

According to Exodus 25:18-20, the cherubim on each end faced one other and looked toward the mercy seat. They had wings of gold that extended above, overshadowing the ark. Leviticus 16:2 says that above this mercy seat was a cloud and God said that He would appear to the priest in the cloud. When we have the visible manifestation of a cloud of glory in our church, it is a manifestation of the presence of the Lord, signifying that the church represents a place where the ark rests; for where the ark is, there is His glory.

Do you remember the story in Second Samuel 6 about David and the ark and how he left it at the home of Obededom? The ark remained there for three months and the Lord blessed Obededom, his household, and all that he had. As we experience God's manifest presence in our midst, we enjoy love, joy, peace, prosperity, and unity like never before. Sometimes it is like Heaven has come down and we are abiding in its atmosphere.

After David saw how the Lord blessed Obededom, he and his chosen men went together to carry the ark to Jerusalem. When the ark was entering the city, Michal, the daughter of Saul, was watching from a window. She could see David going before the ark, leaping, and dancing, and praising the Lord, and she despised David because of his freedom.

David was a king, but there he was, dancing before the Lord with all his might with nothing on but a linen ephod! He was excited about the blessing that the ark would bring back to Jerusalem. He knew that the life was in the ark because it represented the presence of God.

People may wonder why I get a little crazy—it is because of the Lord's presence. There is no reason on earth why I would act the way I do at times, other than and apart from His presence. Psalm 16:11 says, "In Your presence is fullness of joy." The presence of the Lord brings me joy, as the Bible says, "unspeakable and full of glory" (1 Pet. 1:8b KJV).

The ark contains the glory of the Lord, and when you come to the glory you will find forgiveness at the mercy seat. The mercy of God is His kindness and grace revealed to us. And what is grace? It is the unmerited favor of God expressed towards His people. We do not deserve grace and forgiveness, nor do we deserve any second chances. But because Jesus Christ died for the sins of all mankind, He has given us forgiveness, a second chance, freedom, liberty, joy, peace; all these gifts are now ours through our merciful Savior.

The high priest could only behold the presence of the ark of the covenant when he would go in to make atonement for the sins of the people. Before he went into the Holy of Holies, he and the other priests would sacrifice animals because without the shedding of blood there could be no remission of sin. The high priest would actually have to crawl into the Holy of Holies wearing small gold bells that were attached to the hem of his robe.

I have heard of a church in the northeast part of our country that was privileged to witness the presence of the Lord ministering in such a priestly role. The entire congregation was there when a physical manifestation of Jesus appeared, wearing a priestly robe adorned with gold bells. Jesus began to walk up the stairs, departing, and as He did, the pastor cried out, "Lord, if I could just have a bell from Your robe." A little bell fell off the robe and rolled down on the altar area, and the pastor picked up the bell. It was witnessed by hundreds of people. Hallelujah!

The noise of the bells identified the high priest as he crossed through the veil in the tabernacle, so that he would not be mistaken for an unconsecrated person and die. If any priest entered into the Holy Place without proper cleansing, the bells would cease ringing. The silence would indicate to the people in the outer court that the priest had died because he had failed to enter into God's presence as a holy vessel. His body was then removed by a rope that was attached to him.

There was a veil that separated the Holy Place from the Holy of Holies. By Jesus' death on the cross, the veil was torn in two, and now all of us who have been purified by His blood have access to the Holy of Holies. We can all come before the ark and appropriate the mercy seat. The shedding of Christ's blood enacts the purification that God requires of us to enter into His holy presence.

Hebrews 4:16 says, "Let us therefore come boldly to the throne of grace, that we may obtain mercy and find grace to help in time of need." We can come boldly to the very throne of God because of Jesus. What access we have! We have the ability, by faith, to enter into the very presence of God Almighty.

I remember years ago, in the early part of 1973, I was praying; and it was the first time I actually experienced something that just about blew my mind. It was about five o'clock in the morning and I was praying in the church with several other people. It seemed like the Lord would always show up about the same time, and being totally ignorant, we never knew why. We finally figured out that at five a.m. we were completely exhausted and our flesh was at its weakest point.

As we were praying at the altar, suddenly we heard something at the back of the church. The front was dimly lit, but it was dark in the rest of the sanctuary. Then we heard footsteps. We became terrified, and we began to tremble and cry uncontrollably. We were so scared that we could not move our heads to look around.

We sensed an awesome and holy presence walking down the aisle. We discerned quickly that it was not the devil. We could feel and hear something coming. All of a sudden, the Lord came, stopped, and put His hands on our shoulders. We could never turn around and look. All we could do was lie on the floor, crushed by His awesome presence!

When Jesus passes our way He will reveal Himself to us in the Holy Place. But you have got to move out of the outer court to come before the mercy seat, and He will let you enter in. Jesus is the entrance into the Holy Place; His shed blood paves the way. He is the mercy seat that we seek. Under the old covenant, the people did not have the privilege you and I have today. In the old covenant, they could not approach the mercy seat. You can come to the mercy seat anytime you choose, even if you are living in the outer court.

If you will go there, you will find God's presence, which will change you forever. You may say, "I've been living around the ark of the covenant and I'm still the same." But do you know there is more? Do you know that it's impossible to tap in to the resources of God and receive everything He has all at once? Each time you draw from the well and every time you touch the Lord, you will find there is more of Him, more than you will ever be able to contain. There is more of God than we can imagine. His resources are unlimited, and His ability to meet your needs is too.

God is very much into establishing covenant relationships. The ark housed the tables of the covenant that included the tablets God gave Moses on the mount, the Ten Commandments, and the laws that were carried with them. The tables of the covenant represented His Word.

But in the new covenant, God says in Hebrews 10:16, "This is the covenant that I will make with them after those days, says the Lord: I will put My laws into their hearts, and in their minds I will write them." You will discover as you come into the presence of the Lord, you will begin to hear His voice. The living word of God that you hear is called *rhema*. It is not just a word that comes from historical accounts or even through reading the Good Book. You can read the Bible, but unless the Spirit enlightens it, what you read will not be alive to you.

When you hear a *rhema* word, it must always be confirmed with the written Word in the Bible. Many have gone into deception when they stray from the plumb line within the Word of God.

The Word comes from the place called the mercy seat and when God speaks, it only takes a little bit to make a lot of changes. Years ago when we were living out in the country in Iowa, I was at a very low point in my life. I had been involved with a group that didn't work out and because of the circumstances I found myself basically out of the ministry for the first time. I was very frustrated and very convicted.

I know my family still remembers some of the times when they heard me wailing in the middle of the night. The pain was so deep in my spirit that I would cry out to the Lord in the middle of my living room. One day I went out to the edge of the woods that was near our house and found a tree stump. I sat down on the stump and heard the Lord speak. He did not come to me and say, "Open your Bible to the Book of Deuteronomy chapter 1 and read verses 1 through 10 and 20 through 40, and then read this, etc., etc., etc."

But the Lord spoke very plain that day the words that changed my life, "Bill, I still love you." Whew. That's all He said. And He said it clearly. Within two weeks I was back in the ministry—from ground zero back to the pastorate in two weeks.

I was in the carpet cleaning business, and that same week as I dragged my hose into a customer's house in Cedar Rapids, Iowa, I heard Christian music playing. I said, "Uh-oh." At that time I didn't particularly want to be in that atmosphere. I walked up to the door and met a wonderful lady named Joy who happened to be a pastor of a Brethren church. We began our conversation and then she looked at me, pointed at me, and said, "You're a pastor. You are called of God. He loves you."

Everything opened up immediately after that, and I was asked to preach in a little church. All the people who had invited me had come out of the same denomination. There was about 15 or 20 members attending at the time.

I remember that on the first Sunday I preached again, I said, "Lord, if it's really You and You are confirming my call, then I want there to be a manifestation of Your power." As I concluded the Word and began to minister, people began to fall over in the power of God. They were frightened and I was too, because I did not know that the Lord would still display His power through me in such a way.

And it all started when I heard a simple word on a tree stump, "Bill, I still love you." At the mercy seat, you will hear God speak. The Bible says His words are spirit and they are life. When God speaks, you will hear His Word and it will impart life to you. It will bring hope back to a hopeless individual, and it will bring faith to someone who has been captured by the spirit of fear. When the Lord speaks, WOW!

Hebrews 9:4 describes the golden pot of manna that symbolized the sustaining life and strength that the Lord brought. Once God speaks and He breaks you out of your present condition into His provisions, how will you continue to maintain that position? By going back to the pot every day, going back to the place where there is life.

In John 6:56 the Lord said, "He who eats My flesh and drinks My blood abides in Me, and I in him." And in verse 58, "This is the bread which came down from heaven—not as your fathers ate the manna, and are dead. He who eats this bread will live forever." The more you go back, the more you eat of Him. Drink, eat, and take the manna of the Lord that is delivered fresh every day; His mercies are new to you every morning. The more you do that, the more His life is imparted to you.

His life keeps building and building and building within you. You realize that you do not begin fully developed. You do not become all you are supposed to be in just a moment, in just a twinkling of an eye. You begin to have access to all you can be, but it takes a lifetime of manna for you to become the finished product God has intended.

Most people are too impatient to realize that it takes a lifetime for God to transform them into a purified vessel. Don't give up now. If you are in your teens or in your early twenties, you are only at the beginning of something awesome. You are at the beginning of a lifetime of pleasing God. Please the Lord and let God minister to you all of His love. This life is wonderful if you walk with Jesus, but it is most miserable if you choose to walk without Him.

Hebrews 9:4 mentions that Aaron's rod had budded. God placed the rod there symbolically, but it is profound because it represents the priestly anointing that comes to you, and out of that anointing the fruit will begin to manifest.

What separates someone who has the Spirit of Jesus from the person who has a spirit of anger, strife, and conflict in their life? It is the anointing. It's not because one is better than the other, but because the believer who is anointed of the Lord is one who bears His fruit. If you want love, joy, peace, longsuffering, gentleness, goodness, meekness, and faith, then come before the mercy seat and kneel down before the ark of the covenant and begin to bask in the presence of the Lord. He said, "For I will appear in the cloud above the mercy seat" (Lev. 16:2b). We have seen the visible cloud and we know that the Lord is in the midst of us.

All I can be today and all that you can be is just a receptacle. We say, "Lord, here we are. Just pour it into us, more Lord, more, just pour it in." Do you want Him to pour in some more, and how about some more after that, and some more after that? More Lord, more Lord, more Lord—pour it in, pour it in.

God wants to do miracles and be the miracles in your life. He wants to be your miracle source without exception. The Lord loves you, and His joy comes by giving you His eternal rewards. He is here because of His sacrifice on the cross. The most perfect man who ever lived, Jesus, the Son of God, went to a cross with your sins on His back. The Bible says that He became your sin bearer. He took all your sins and He died so that you could live.

He was raised so that you could be raised with Him and He was seated at the right hand of God so that you could be with Him. Let the mercy of the Lord be your portion and let the anointing of God come upon you, transforming you into His Holy presence. This is the hour that God's power can be released upon your life. If you allow Him to, He will impart something supernatural in your life today.

There is a mercy seat waiting for you and there is a cloud of glory waiting, so come boldly to the throne of grace in your time of need. The Lord is saying, "You will find help there."

If you do not know Jesus, just remember this: It is not difficult to know Him. All you have to do is open your heart to Him to be born again. Realize that you are a sinner and that nothing you can do can merit favor with God. If you will simply say, "Lord Jesus, forgive me of my sins, come into my heart and cleanse me from my unrighteousness," the Lord said He would be faithful to come into you, and to forgive you, and to cleanse you from all unrighteousness.

Psalm 103:12 says, "As far as the east is from the west, so far has He removed our transgressions from us." You can be free! Where the Spirit of the Lord is, there is liberty. The Lord wants to do something special in your life today. If you have been living in the outer court and you are tired of existing on the fringe, just say,

"Today, Lord, I want to enter the holy place by the blood of Jesus and I want to take up residence there." His glory will come in and touch the life of anyone who hungers and thirsts for Him.

CHAPTER 5

The Pathway to Glory

One of the most important aspects of our physical life is proper positioning. In other words, being at the right place at the right time. That counts for a lot, doesn't it? How many times have you thought about your life and realized that if you had missed a certain flight, or taken a trip other than the one you originally planned, or not applied for that certain job, your life would have turned out differently?

If I hadn't gone to the local Denny's restaurant in October of 1968, and met a beautiful young woman, my life would have been entirely different. Back then I was writing a lot of poetry instead of going to my college classes. During the day I would lie out by the pool at our apartment and write. Eventually I told my dad about it, but at that time he thought I was studying.

My best friend hoodwinked me into going to the Denny's. He said, "Can you take time out from writing long enough to go to Denny's restaurant and have some coffee?" It was a Sunday night and little did I know I was going to meet a church girl. That was the last thing on my mind. I met her that October and by January we were married. How my life would have turned out differently if I hadn't been at that Denny's. I was at the right place at the right time.

So our circumstances are determined by proper positioning. Being at the right or wrong place, the right or wrong time, determines the outcome of our life. That's why, at our church, we counsel our young people to be careful who they date, because whoever they date could become their potential mate. Second Corinthians

6:14 says, "Do not be unequally yoked together with unbelievers. For what fellowship has righteousness with lawlessness? And what communion has light with darkness?" If you yoke yourself with someone who does not have a heart for the Lord, your life will be filled with continual challenges. Exercising your faith according to the way that God directs your heart will be a constant uphill battle.

Worship also involves proper positioning. When we properly position our worship before God, He then reveals Himself according to the position of our heart. Worship is designed to not only adore and exalt the Lord to His rightful place, seated at the right hand of the Father, but worship is by nature that which invokes the presence of God into our midst.

As we gather at our church for our Friday night manifestation meetings, most of us realize the significance and awesomeness of being able to witness the glory cloud with our naked eyes. We have found that there is a direct correlation between our praise that comes forth and the thickness and heaviness of the glory cloud that appears. The density changes with the intensity of worship that flows from our hearts.

We usually start our Friday service with everyone praying or worshiping as individuals and often we will have soft praise music playing. It is during this time that we search our hearts and get our spirits in tune with the Lord. When the Holy Spirit leads us, we then gather at the altar in front of the pulpit and begin to worship together. We never seek a manifestation during this time but are always humbled and blessed when there is a visible appearance of the cloud of glory.

Now, in order to be a proper worshiper, you must be in the proper position. You assume humility as the first position. Humility is when you acknowledge that there is someone and something greater than yourself.

Pride is the greatest sin against the Lord because a prideful individual assumes he has life's destiny in his own hands. But pride leads us down a road of destruction. Humility comes through repentance and brings us into a position where God can lead our lives and control that which is about to happen.

Do you want to be in charge of your own life? That is a loaded question. You really do not want to be, because you know that if you are left in charge, your life will wind up in ruin. As the Bible says in First Corinthians 6:19-20, "Or do you not know that your body is the temple of the Holy Spirit who is in you, whom you have from God, and you are not your own? For you were bought at a price; therefore glorify God in your body and in your spirit, which are God's."

The greatest mark of maturity is when you surrender your life to someone greater who has more wisdom and understanding, and more knowledge of your past, present, and future than you do. That someone is the Lord. To acknowledge Him as Lord means to surrender your will to Him. This is a free-will offering that we must give daily. It is not something that is coerced out of us because we fear God and think He is a mean dictator.

God is not mean; He loves us and wants us to surrender our will to Him so that we are able to lead fruitful lives and multiply the spiritual seeds that He has planted within us. The greatest legacy that any of you can leave after you are buried in a box, cremated, or taken up is that during your lifetime, Christ was multiplied and duplicated within you.

The nature of the Lord is revealed through your life, because what we are, both in this generation and if there are generations to come, is building blocks for the Kingdom. Everything that is within us has an eternal ramification, either for the good or bad. When we allow the Holy Spirit to fill us and lead us, we become building blocks for something that is greater yet to come.

Everything we are doing in the Body of Christ throughout the earth is preparing a place for the Lord to inhabit. God's intention,

His will and His purpose, is that one day the glory of the Lord will fill the whole earth and that it will come through His people.

Isaiah was a prophet who spoke about the wonders of the coming Kingdom. In Isaiah 60:1-2, he said, "Arise, shine; for your light has come! And the glory of the Lord is risen upon you. For behold, the darkness shall cover the earth, and deep darkness the people; but the Lord will arise over you, and His glory will be seen upon you."

We are seeing that happening now, not only in our own territory, but we are seeing it throughout the earth. There is a resurgence of emphasizing the glory because that is where the focus must be. The glory represents God in our midst.

I was watching a television program where they broadcasted an exorcism in which the minister spent 25 hours getting a demon out of a person. There is nothing wrong with that, but you know, it can happen a lot quicker. I used to spend all day and all night working with someone. I have watched demons come out of people; I have had strange growling voices talk to me and have had the experience of a 110-pound woman needing five people to hold her down. But that is not necessary if you know that your authority is in Christ.

The one thing that was significant on this television program was a clip of the host talking to the pastor in a separate interview. At one point they were discussing God's sense of humor, and in the middle of their conversation, suddenly they heard a loud clap of thunder! The pastor just smiled because it was obviously a demonstration of the Lord right there in the middle of an interview on a network news program. You couldn't deny it. It was awesome!

God wants to demonstrate Himself to the earth, and more and more we are going to see that even the news media will begin to pick up stories on the glory and demonstration of the Lord's power. That program was the first time I have seen a report from a national television network that didn't convey a lot of negativity against deliverance and more or less supported what was taking place.

Even a psychiatrist from the American Psychiatric Association was there, who supported the principle of deliverance and the existence of demonic possession.

Our focus here is not demonic possession; our focus is on the glory of the Lord.

> *When Solomon had finished praying, fire came down from heaven and consumed the burnt offering and the sacrifices; and the glory of the Lord filled the temple. And the priests could not enter the house of the Lord, because the glory of the Lord had filled the Lord's house. When all the children of Israel saw how the fire came down, and the glory of the Lord on the temple, they bowed their faces to the ground on the pavement, and worshiped and praised the Lord, saying: 'For He is good, for His mercy endures forever.' Then the king and all the people offered sacrifices before the Lord. King Solomon offered a sacrifice of twenty-two thousand bulls and one hundred and twenty thousand sheep. So the king and all the people dedicated the house of God. And the priests attended to their services; the Levites also with instruments of the music of the Lord, which King David had made to praise the Lord, saying, 'For His mercy endures forever,' whenever David offered praise by their ministry. The priests sounded trumpets opposite them, while all Israel stood* (2 Chronicles 7:1-6).

The children of Israel positioned themselves through an act of obedience and consequently the Lord filled the house with His glory. Hebrews 9 teaches us about the tabernacle. As I said before there are three courts: the outer court, the inner court (the Holy Place), and the Holy of Holies. The holy court is the place that represents our position in Christ. Some are on the outside, some on the inside, and some in the most intimate place.

And so it holds true that our hearts can be in one of three positions: We can either be observing that which is taking place, we can be close to it, or we can be where it is actually happening. God wants to draw each one of us into His inner court where we can have an actual experience with Him—not as those who hear about Him or observe Him from a distance, but as those who can see and be with Him up close.

One time at our church, after we had again witnessed a manifestation of the glory cloud, an individual pointed out to me that when certain individuals departed the service, the glory instantly became stronger. The Lord will not allow those who have hearts that are not right to witness His presence and His glory. Even though God might appear, they will still deny it because their hearts are not right. Even when God physically manifests His glory they will be skeptical.

They are like the apostle Thomas. He saw everything yet he was still skeptical. He did not really believe. "Then [Jesus] said to Thomas, 'Reach your finger here, and look at My hands; and reach your hand here, and put it into My side. Do not be unbelieving, but believing.' And Thomas answered and said to Him, 'My Lord and my God!' Jesus said to him, 'Thomas, because you have seen Me, you have believed. Blessed are those who have not seen and yet have believed' " (John 20: 27-29).

The Lord says the way into the glory is through worship. Psalm 100:4 says, "Enter into His gates with thanksgiving, and into His courts with praise. Be thankful to Him, and bless His name." As we learn to worship the Lord, we understand that the key ingredient to worship is surrendering our will. You must will yourself to worship; you must determine to love the Lord; and you must set yourself and your affections upon the Lord.

Your will is a part of your soul. The human being is made up of a soul, a spirit, and a body. Of course, most people in the natural world live only by what feels good, tastes good, and sounds good.

They live for what gives them temporary self-satisfaction. Consequently, most people go from one drug to the next, one illicit relationship to the next, and from one experience to the next, always seeking—which simply proves that those things do not bring sustaining satisfaction.

You cannot find true and lasting satisfaction in sex, alcohol and drugs, nor in vacations or job experiences; those things provide only temporal satisfaction. True satisfaction cannot come to the flesh; and the harder we strive to satisfy our flesh, the more frustrated we will become. True satisfaction can only be found when the inner man is made alive to God.

Every person has something within that cries out for the Lord. That desire is what drew all of us to Him to start with, wasn't it? I was not brought up spiritual; I was brought up in religion. I was not raised to be what I am today. I became what I am because of the hunger inside my heart for something greater. God has put that hunger in every man.

In each lifetime, everyone has opportunities to make the choice to serve the Lord, but many choose not to. They either accept or reject Him. Jesus said in John 1:12, "But as many as received Him, to them He gave the right to become children of God, to those who believe in His name."

If we reject the Word, God will not constrain us to accept Him; He gives us free choice. Your will is your free moral agent to determine where you are going to be found in Christ and what your life is going to become. Your will is a part of your being that can overcome your mind and emotions. The Bible says in Romans 8:7, "Because the carnal mind is enmity against God; for it is not subject to the law of God, nor indeed can be." In other words, the mind of man does not think the thoughts of God, nor cherish them. The mind of man is seeking its own satisfaction, and as we progress in years, the variety and level of that insatiable hunger increases.

A child, a young man, a mature man, and an elderly man each have different priorities in the natural. The older you become the more you pursue security. The younger you are, the more you pursue fun, fun, fun. We think that the more fun we experience the happier we will be. But the next day we always wake up and find that temporal feeling didn't suffice, so we continue to look for a new experience.

When I was growing up, there were not a lot of fast food restaurants in our town. In the '50s and early '60s it was a big treat to just be able to go to the drive-in and get a hamburger every now and then. It was a thrill to get out of the house and go to this little place in Muleshoe, Texas called the Corral. We would usually order a hamburger or burrito to eat. Nowadays young people don't get much of a thrill just by getting out of the house and going for a hamburger. They've got to have something more than that to get excited about.

The more "things" we acquire on the soulish level, the less satisfied we are. Our whole world is now filled with enticing advertisments and technology. The big question on kids' minds today is which latest model video game player will they buy this year. And after they get one they ask, "Which one do I want next?" There is something inside of us that wants to have more and more fun; and usually the younger we are, the more we care about having fun.

When we get older and become responsible for things like marriage and children, our priorities should change. There really is a problem when someone gets married and has children, and the husband or wife still only wants to pursue fun. Our human nature and its desire for fulfillment is not something that will ever truly be satisfied. It is only in your spiritual man that you will find fulfillment and your destiny.

It is when you begin to live your life for something greater than yourself that you really begin to live. Life begins when you begin to live for others. We are merely existing on experiences until we learn to put others first. When we become selfless, life becomes truly enjoyable and fruitful. When our motivation is to be a blessing to the earth, then and only then are we beginning to behave like Jesus. Many people are looking for prosperity and happiness in life, and they could enjoy both blessings if they would walk in this principle.

I am an easy crier. If I see something sentimental on television or at the movies I'll sit there and the tears will start to flow. Sometimes that will also happen when I'm sitting around thinking about how I can bless other people. I will start crying because my greatest joy now comes from thinking of how I can be a blessing on this earth. What can I do to sow myself into God's creation so that His Kingdom prospers and souls may be saved and lives changed?

I am not declaring that I am a saint. I am saying that as we go further in Christ, our will should be conformed to the point that we have overcome the flesh and the mind, which is enmity against God. We must allow the spiritual man to rule in our life. You do not have to allow your flesh and your emotions to rule; you can let Christ reign in your life.

Now when you begin to seek first the Kingdom of God and His righteousness, then Jesus says in Matthew 6:33, "...all these things shall be added to you." You start to have fun again and enjoy the fruit of life once you have learned the meaning of life. But to try and enjoy the fruit before you have learned the meaning only brings a life that is premature and empty.

Our will is so powerful that it has the ability to determine if we will be a worshiper or a blasphemer, a lover of God or a hater of God. Once we have accepted Christ into our life we must begin the journey of setting ourselves to be true worshipers of the Lord. We must daily be worshiping and seeking the Lord to allow His understanding and His wisdom to prevail within us.

The Lord gives us the Holy Spirit who then becomes a conduit and an instrument by which we can go beyond our understanding, beyond our ability in the natural to become a worshiper of the Lord.

Jesus said in John 4:24, "...and those who worship Him must worship in spirit and truth." The Spirit takes us away from practicing religious exercises and moves us into a position of anointing where there is actual communion taking place between the Lord and ourselves.

We can instantly go before the throne of God. Hebrews 4:16 says, "Let us therefore come boldly to the throne of grace, that we may obtain mercy and find grace to help in time of need." We can pray for the anointing right now and be caught up into another realm, even while we are in the world. Remember, we are in the world, but not of the world. We have another source of supply.

I can listen to His voice as I am speaking to someone or preaching, and you can do the same. It is so amazing; sometimes after I preach a message, someone will come up to me and say, "That message really spoke to me." Then they will begin to tell me what God was speaking to them through the message. They had obviously heard the Lord, because I had not preached one word of what they said that they had heard.

You see, if the one who is speaking the Word of the Lord is anointed, then you will hear on the level or at the place of your greatest need. God will take the words and make them spirit and life. They are not natural words and they are not intended to speak to your flesh; they are intended to speak directly to your spiritual man.

Someone's interpretation of what I am saying may be different from my actual words; this is a confirmation of how the Lord works. Some need milk, some bread, and some meat. You don't get up to preach and try to make the message so simple that it's like, "Mary had a little lamb"—as if everybody needs milk. When you speak under the anointing, the Lord will minister to the different levels of the needs. Some will drink milk during the message, some will eat bread, and some will eat meat.

At this point there should be a quickening in your spirit from the Lord through what I am teaching you. There could be a conflict in you between that which is your own desire and that which is the desire of the Lord. He begins to separate the precious from the vile that is within you, to separate the will of man from the will of God. Hebrews 4:12 says, "For the word of God is living and powerful, and sharper than any two-edged sword, piercing even to the division of soul and spirit, and of joints and marrow, and is a discerner of the thoughts and intents of the heart."

It is important to saturate yourself in the Word, because the Word comes like water that cleanses you. How would you like to go a whole week never taking a bath or a shower? How would you like to go a month or a year? You can tell which people go a long time without hearing the Word because they begin to stink. Their attitudes are sorry; their hearts are hard; and they are bitter, resentful, envious, jealous, greedy, lustful, and full of strife.

Sins begin to breed when the human spirit quits hearing the Word of the Lord. We begin to revert back to the pit that we have been dug out of. We begin to return to where the hogs slop. If you have ever been around hogs, you know that it is a very nasty place to be. Those old hogs get in there and just wallow around in the mud and the slop. And if you throw a bucket of slop in their pen, they'll eat right out of the mud and even eat excrement right along with their food.

And that is human nature, to go right back into the vile place that we have come out of. It is only in the Word that we can maintain a place of purity in our hearts. The Word has the power to sustain us, and even at that, it is difficult sometimes. Even if you saturate yourself in the Word, the gravitational pull of the world is so strong, it is difficult to stay out of the slop hole that God has brought us out of.

We must keep exposing ourselves to the Lord. Psalm 139:23-24 says, "Search me, O God, and know my heart; try me, and know my anxieties; and see if there is any wicked way in me, and lead me in the way everlasting." The Lord said the Word will come, and we have a choice when it comes; we can either fall upon the Word and be broken by it, or the Word will fall upon us and crush us. What choice have you made?

We are going to see a day come like those times in the Old Testament. The nation of Israel fearlessly marched into foreign lands as the Lord commanded them to annihilate their enemies. God said He did not want anyone in their midst who didn't submit to His will. That case will also be true in the days before the Kingdom. The Bible talks about how many will be slain to the left and to the right. The day will come that the arrogance of man will not be able to resist the will of God.

People today flaunt their atheism or agnostic position and their hatred of God, but the day will come when men will no longer flaunt themselves against the Lord. Philippians 2:10-11 says, "That at the name of Jesus every knee should bow, of those in heaven, and of those on earth, and of those under the earth, and that every tongue should confess that Jesus Christ is Lord, to the glory of God the Father."

The mercy of God is great towards us. He has given us the opportunity to make the right choice at the right time, and we must make the commitment to serve the Lord. There was no one more headstrong or self-determined and self-willed than the man I was. But in 1970, I encountered God in the backyard of my house in Amarillo, Texas. I did not encounter Him in a church; I encountered Him in my backyard. At that moment, I surrendered to the Lord. It has been a hard struggle ever since. God has been whipping me up one side and down the other, because "for whom the Lord loves He chastens, and scourges every son whom He receives" (Heb. 12:6).

God does not discipline us because He hates us; He loves us. A prophecy came to me years ago that I was going to become an

"Israel," which means a prince of God. The problem was that before Israel was called Israel, his name was Jacob. He was a supplanter, stubborn, one that resisted the will of God. But one night the Lord wrestled with Jacob, and after He was through with him, the Lord left a mark upon Jacob and he limped. Jacob was a different man after that encounter. He became Israel, the prince of God. And like his grandfather Abram who became Abraham, he was transformed by the presence of God and the anointing of the Lord.

Here we learn that God's purpose for the glory is to transform us and give us a new identity. He has given us our will and the opportunity to make a decision to change. There ought to be great humility in us as the glory appears, a brokenness before the Lord, so that we might be like David and say, "But my eyes are upon You, O God the Lord; in You I take refuge" (Ps. 141:8a).

We can fulfill the Lord's commandment in Mark 12:30, "And you shall love the Lord your God with all your heart, with all your soul, with all your mind, and with all your strength." We can be the ones who so love the Lord because we have met Him face to face. In Matthew 18:20, Jesus says, "Where two or three are gathered together in My name, I am there in the midst of them."

We can become the generation that says, "Eye has not seen, nor ear heard, nor have entered into the heart of man the things which God has prepared for those who love Him" (1 Cor. 2:9). We can be those people who become carriers of the glory, not seeking the things of the earth, but the things of the Kingdom.

What separates someone who is average from someone who is above average? It is the glory of the Kingdom in them. It is not their intellect, their looks, or their money; it is the glory. But few people are willing to forsake the temporal pleasures of sin for the eternal weight of glory. I do not know if I am willing, but I seek to overcome the obstacles and possess that sacrificial kind of mind-set. I have not yet met a person who has completely forsaken the things of this world for the glories of the Lord. But there is a remnant, there is a company of people who are seeking, and because of those whom God is calling out, there will be a breakthrough.

In Second Chronicles 5 we learn about the Feast of Tabernacles. It says in verses 3-5, "Therefore all the men of Israel assembled with the king at the feast, which was in the seventh month. So all the elders of Israel came, and the Levites took up the ark. Then they brought up the ark, the tabernacle of meeting, and all the holy furnishings that were in the tabernacle. The priests and the Levites brought them up."

The ark of the covenant was the place where the Word dwelt, symbolizing that that was where all life resided. The life was in the ark and the ark was always accompanied by the glory. You do not have to watch *Raiders of the Lost Ark* to know that to be true. And over the ark were carved cherubim, which were overlaid with gold.

Let's read on in verses 5-7:

> *Then they brought up the ark, the tabernacle of meeting, and all the holy furnishings that were in the tabernacle. The priests and the Levites brought them up. Also King Solomon, and all the congregation of Israel who were assembled with him before the ark, were sacrificing sheep and oxen that could not be counted or numbered for multitude. Then the priests brought in the ark of the covenant of the Lord to its place, into the inner sanctuary of the temple, to the Most Holy Place, under the wings of the cherubim.*

Where did the ark belong? It belonged in the inner sanctuary of the temple. Now what does the New Testament say that the temple is? Second Corinthians 6:16 says, "For you are the temple of the living God." And in Ephesians 2:22, "...in whom you also are being built together for a dwelling place of God in the Spirit." So when you look for the Church, do you look for brick and mortar, or in the case of our church, a blue metal building? No, you look to the one sitting next to you. The Church is in you, in your brother, your sister, your wife, your husband. They are where you will find the tabernacle, and inside them is where the glory dwells.

Second Corinthians 3:3 says, "Clearly you are an epistle of Christ, ministered by us, written not with ink but by the Spirit of the living God, not on tablets of stone but on tablets of flesh, that is, of the heart." If the Word represents the life inside the ark, then the Word that is written upon our hearts, inside the ark that is within us, is the life. Christ in you is the hope of glory. The ark is within you and the glory is resident within all those who have heard the Word and have let that Word be etched and written upon their hearts.

The ark and the glory are not in everyone who says, "Hey, I'm a Christian," but the ones who have said, "Be it done unto me according to Thy Word." They stick their heart out and say, "Lord, here is my heart; write Your Word upon it that out of my belly shall flow rivers of living water." This water is the Word coming forth.

The greater the yielding in worship to the Lord, the more the Word can be engraved upon your heart. Consequently, out of that transference to you, comes forth the transference from you. The rivers that will water the earth are coming forth from you.

Jeremiah 20:9b says, "His word was in my heart like a burning fire shut up in my bones...." The living Word has got to come out. We are repeatedly going to be imprinted and impregnated with the Word until that is all we have left within us. We will be consumed by the Word of the Lord and ultimately become "...known and read by all men...a [letter] of Christ...written not with ink but by the Spirit of the living God..." (2 Cor. 3:2-3).

John 1:1 says, "In the beginning was the Word, and the Word was with God, and the Word was God." And in John 1:14a, "And the Word became flesh and dwelt among us, and we beheld His glory." It is the same principle and our ultimate destiny; we are going to become the manifestation of the Word. When the people looked at Jesus, they could not separate Him from the Word that He spoke, as Jesus said, "But the Father who sent Me gave Me a command, what I should say and what I should speak" (Jn. 12:49b). And Jesus said in John 10:30, "I and My Father are one."

And so we too must become those who are not separated from His voice or from His Word. Out of our hearts come forth the words of life. Isaiah 35:6b says, "For waters shall burst forth in the wilderness, and streams in the desert." This Word will be fulfilled, because the word that comes out of us is making a pathway for others. You have the power of life and death in your tongue. You can speak a pathway of victory for someone who is living in defeat. You can prophesy. Where the Spirit of Christ is, there is the spirit of prophecy.

To prophesy into a person's life is as easy as breathing. The Lord wants to bless people and He wants to use you to be His channel. Ask the Lord to give you His love for someone and then open your mouth to bless them. The Holy Spirit will give you the words to encourage and uplift them. You will be amazed at how little you have to say to make a difference in someone's life.

You can prophesy life to someone and make a way in the wilderness for the one who is lost. You can bring them to a river of living water in the middle of the desert. Glory to God! So we cry out, "Lord, let Your anointing come, let Your Word be so deep within us that it cannot be separated from us."

Second Chronicles 5:7 says, "Then the priests brought in the ark of the covenant of the Lord to its place, into the inner sanctuary of the temple, to the Most Holy Place, under the wings of the cherubim." Now where is the Most Holy Place? "Under the wings of the cherubim."

When the glory cloud came into our church I asked, "What does this represent?" And the Lord said, "It represents My presence over the ark." So our church building is a type and a shadow of the ark, and the glory of the Lord is confirming what is taking place within our hearts. That makes our church a very holy place. If someone comes into our building and starts doing something in the flesh, I will move them right out because I honor this place as holy.

The manifestations that we are seeing are important representations of what is happening within us. In the old covenant everything began without and was observed from an outer position. In the New Testament it all begins within but ultimately is expressed outwardly. What is within us is eventually going to come out, and our fruit, whether good or bad, is going to be exposed. What is being done in secret is going to be revealed to all, whether it is evil or righteous. Thank God for His grace when that happens.

In the old covenant the Lord would deal primarily with the outward man; in the new covenant the Lord transforms the heart or spirit of man. The ultimate glory that will be revealed is the appearance of the Lord Jesus Christ Himself at the Second Coming. He will come back where every eye will see Him. But first He is establishing a Kingdom within His people.

The Lord showed me that the altar in the church represents the ark and this is where the Word comes forth. Second Chronicles 5:8 says, "For the cherubim spread their wings over the place of the ark, and the cherubim overshadowed the ark and its poles." Above the ark was a cloud and the Lord said in Exodus 19:9, "I come to you in the thick cloud."

When I preached this message there was a great manifestation that took place, and we all fell back in the Spirit. It was just like in First Kings 8:11, where it says they could not stand when the glory came in. We were all filled with the Spirit and were so drunk in the Spirit that we could not even walk. Some would say that the term "drunk" minimizes the experience. But how else can you describe it? When you are drunk with alcohol, your body no longer responds the way you would choose for it to.

It is the same when the anointing comes and we get drunk in the Spirit. Our natural body is rendered ineffective. Acts 2:15 says, "For these are not drunk, as you suppose, since it is only the third hour of the day." And in Acts 2:4 the explanation for their behavior is: "And they were all filled with the Holy Spirit." That is what occurred on the day of Pentecost, and that is what is happening again today.

We witnessed the cloud right above our heads the moment I began to share about the glory cloud from the Word. We all saw it with our eyes and fell backwards under the glory. It was awesome! You see, the Lord is returning the glory to the house but it rests over the ark, over the Word. The Lord showed me that the reason the glory is coming here in this manner is because of what is being spoken. Do you think the glory would be coming to a place where something other than the Kingdom was being preached?

In 1987 a man of God named Rick Godwin from San Antonio came to Austin to preach at one of our evening services. We were then meeting in our old building. Rick was a great preacher from the start, and at that time he was coming into a greater awareness of the deeper callings of the Spirit. He came into our service, walked up to the front, and began to prophesy to me. Later he told me I was the first person he had ever prophesied to.

He prophesied that many times in our church we have tried to follow other men, have tried to bring other words, and have tried to imitate others' patterns in order to bring forth what God wanted. But the Lord was going to give us a word that was unique to the Body of Christ. Over the years that prophecy kept coming back to haunt me. We as a church grew large and began initiating the "latest and greatest" church growth programs of the day.

We began to investigate personality profiles to try to find out where everybody fit into specific ministries. However, we learned that you cannot take personality profiles in the natural and try to become a spiritual church with a formula construed from the mind of man. You have to let the Holy Spirit lead and develop an individual's ministry.

We ventured in several different directions and after all was said and done, we wound up in "frustration city." So finally after years of striving to accomplish what I was learning by attending conferences and reading all the how-to books, I just quit. I quit going here and there and quit reading about what other churches were doing to become "successful." I finally just gave up trying to build the church using man's methods and decided to let go and let God. "Unless the Lord builds the house, they labor in vain who build it" (Ps. 127:1a).

And the Lord told me, "Don't worry about the numbers right now; just focus on My glory. When the glory comes, you don't have to worry about the numbers. Whatever numbers come will be up to Me." If He wants two, or 200, or 2000, or 20,000, or 200,000; it's not my concern. The moment you start counting the numbers is the moment you have reverted back to the flesh.

So if there are 10 people in our church on Wednesday nights, or 20, or 30, or 40, I don't worry; I still preach like there are 20,000 people there. Whether there are 50, or 100, or 500 at church on Sunday morning, I don't worry. I will preach like it is a full coliseum. The issue is not how many people are present; the issue is the glory. Jesus said in Matthew 16:18b, "And on this rock I will build My church, and the gates of Hades shall not prevail against it." It is the Lord's house; it is not for me to number those who are in "Israel" and to evaluate my success by the standards of other people.

After much resistance from my own spirit over the years, the Lord finally got my attention. He revealed to me that the unique calling placed on our church is to establish a Word that will bring the glory. The reason the glory cloud is in our church is not because anyone here is righteous or holy enough to see it or because we are praying more or we are doing something greater than anyone else is doing. That's not the issue. The only reason the glory cloud is coming is because the Lord is confirming His Word with signs and wonders. He is saying, "You're on the right track, keep speaking it."

The Word that has been spoken in our church is a kind and merciful Word, but it is not popular. It does not appeal to the natural mind; it does not titillate or stir up the flesh of man to make you all excited, even though we get very excited. It is not how to become successful in the flesh, even though you can become very successful through the Word that is spoken.

This Word is not intended to blow my own horn. It is not me proclaiming this Word. It is what God is speaking. I am simply a vessel trying to yield myself to the Holy Spirit so that the Lord can bring forth His Kingdom in our midst. That is exactly what He wants to do, and that is exactly what He will do if we will only yield to Him. The Lord wants to do a lot more with us than what we have already experienced.

> *Then the priests brought in the ark of the covenant of the Lord to its place, into the inner sanctuary of the temple, to the Most Holy Place, under the wings of the cherubim. For the cherubim spread their wings over the place of the ark, and the cherubim overshadowed the ark and its poles. The poles extended so that the ends of the poles of the ark could be seen from the holy place, in front of the inner sanctuary; but they could not be seen from outside. And they are there to this day* (2 Chronicles 5:7-9).

Again this Scripture emphasizes that unless you are in the middle of God's glory, you will not be able to experience Him for yourself. You can be close and still not see.

Second Chronicles goes on to say in verses 10-12,

> *Nothing was in the ark except the two tablets which Moses put there at Horeb, when the Lord made a covenant with the children of Israel, when they had come out of Egypt. And it came to pass when the priests came out of the Most Holy Place (for all the*

priests who were present had sanctified themselves, without keeping to their divisions), and the Levites who were the singers, all those of Asaph and Heman and Jeduthun, with their sons and their brethren, stood at the east end of the altar, clothed in white linen, having cymbals, stringed instruments and harps, and with them one hundred and twenty priests sounding with trumpets (2 Chronicles 5:10-12).

The New Testament says, "...stand fast in one spirit, with one mind striving together for the faith of the gospel" (Phil. 1:27). The gospel of the Kingdom is not up for debate. We cannot dilute the Kingdom message with the plans and good intentions of man by trying to teach a different gospel. The Church is seriously grieving the Holy Spirit by preaching a different gospel.

According to the New Testament, the gospel of the Kingdom is not one of easy believe-ism. It is not the gospel of user-friendly-ism or self-helps. It is not the gospel of how to achieve your own agenda. It is the gospel of His Kingdom. Until this gospel is preached to all the earth, the glory of the Lord remains restrained. But once the gospel of the Kingdom is expressed based on what God says, then He will reveal His glory to those who are seeking the Spirit and the Truth.

In the church, we want to help married couples, teenagers, the elderly, and all those with needs, but the way to genuinely help them comes through the gospel of the Kingdom. You do not have to address specific needs in order to have victory; needs are addressed in the preaching of the gospel of the Kingdom. You may preach Ephesians 5:22, "Wives, submit to your own husbands, as to the Lord," and in verse 25, "Husbands, love your wives, just as Christ also loved the church and gave Himself for her."

Are those Scriptures the gospel of the Kingdom? No, they are the gospel of the church. Submission to and love for the Lord brings true obedience. We do not have to preach about submission in itself and isolate it. Submission comes because of the authority established through surrendering to His lordship.

> *Indeed it came to pass, when the trumpeters and singers were as one, to make one sound to be heard in praising and thanking the Lord, and when they lifted up their voice with the trumpets and cymbals and instruments of music, and praised the Lord, saying: "For He is good, For His mercy endures forever," that the house, the house of the Lord, was filled with a cloud, so that the priests could not continue ministering because of the cloud; for the glory of the Lord filled the house of God* (2 Chronicles 5:13-14).

We keep praising Him, declaring His victory, declaring His Word, until His glory becomes so prevalent in our midst that even we cannot continue to invoke Him by our practices that have formerly brought the glory. That is called getting overwhelmed in the Spirit. I like it, I love it, and I want some more of it. It is that cry that we have had in our church for years now. We cry out, "More, Lord, give us more of Your glory, more of Your Spirit, more of Your manifestations! Let us see the glory!"

Almost 30 years ago I saw the glory for the first time, and then I went through a wilderness experience. Shortly thereafter I wondered, After all these years will the glory come back? Will the presence and the manifestations happen again? They have happened again, and they are becoming stronger. I do not know what the future holds; but I do know this: I only want to be found in His presence.

Even if at times He doesn't reveal His presence for the natural eye to see, that is all right. We walk by faith not by sight because we know we are on the right road. We are on the road to victory. Do you want that victory in your life? You must become a worshiper. Submit yourself unto God, resist the devil and he will flee from you, realizing that the worshiper, the man of humility, possesses everything.

The Lord said in Isaiah 57:15, "For thus says the High and Lofty One who inhabits eternity, whose name is Holy: 'I dwell in the high and holy place, with him who has a contrite and humble spirit, to revive the spirit of the humble, and to revive the heart of the contrite ones.'"

The Lord lives and He wants to bring us out of the frustration of the flesh. You know, I love riding my motorcycle, but no matter how much I ride, no matter how many hilly country roads I traverse and birds I see flying through the air and flowers I smell and no matter how much joy I receive from going around a sharp curve, none of those things suffice.

I love to travel, to see the bright lights and the oceans and mountains. But when I have been gone for awhile from the house of the Lord and then return, the moment I walk into our church His presence comes, and I think, "Oh, that travel was fun and all those sights I saw were beautiful, but it doesn't even compare to this. All that I have seen and what I've experienced doesn't even compare." And I will begin to cry and say, "My goodness, happy is he that dwells in the house of the Lord."

We will accomplish a lot of things in life, but nothing compares to being in the Father's house. You still have to live your life, but nothing compares to being in the presence of the Lord and in the glory of God. Nothing compares with Jesus.

Thirty years ago He became my Savior; He became my Lord; and most important of all, He became my most intimate friend. I will never forget when, back in 1989, I was caught up to stand with Jesus. I looked in His eyes and felt the love that came forth out of them. It was the most pure, holy experience of my life. I said, "Lord, I'm not worthy to be in Your presence." Silently He communicated, "Yes, I know you're not." But then He spoke these words out loud,

"But you're My friend; I know you're not worthy. I know that you don't deserve to be here, but you're here because you're My friend."

I don't know what Jesus saw in me, but I was humbled because I know that within my flesh dwells no good thing. I have been rebellious, cantankerous, and downright ornery in my natural man. I have lied, cheated, squandered, rebelled, and kicked against His will as much as any man can, yet when it comes right down to it, all I can think of today is what a friend I have in Him.

CHAPTER 6

Our Day of Rejoicing

It is God's will and desire that each one of us go beyond the veil and enter into the Holy Place of God. That is where He speaks His Word. We have looked at three types of worshipers: outer court, inner court, (the Holy Place,) and the Holiest of all, (the Holy of Holies). When you worship the Lord, you have a choice as to what level of worship you participate in. When you go to the worship service at your church, you go because you choose to go, do you not? Does someone make you go? No, you go by exercising your own free will.

Life is full of decisions and the ones we make determine the future of our life. If you make enough right choices enough times, your life will fall in place. If you make enough wrong choices, then you will go down the wrong path and your life will fall apart.

Have you ever heard of people being trapped by their circumstances? When you make the right choices and your will gets involved, you can transcend your circumstances. God gives you power over things around you. He really does. His power in you is greater than that which is without. So we have been given the authority and power to control the destiny of our lives.

It might not always work out in the sequence the way we anticipated. But if we exercise the proper choices, we will have the proper outcome, for right responses will inevitably create right results. If you do something right habitually and consistently long enough, it will always result in right responses and then right results.

The choice to worship is ours and worship is where it's at, because it is in the environment of worship that you can begin to hear the Holy Spirit. If you are reading this book to hear me, Bill Hart, you are going to be sorely disappointed in what is being said. You might gain a tidbit here and there that could seem beneficial to you, but the only real benefit you will receive from reading this book is when the Holy Spirit speaks to you. Listen, and when He speaks to you, it will be life changing and life building.

The Lord adds to the Kingdom line upon line, precept upon precept, a little here, a little there. Every time the Lord speaks there is an increase that takes place in our lives. Jesus Christ is the cornerstone of the house, and we are being built upon the foundation of the words that come forth from the apostles and prophets.

The word that you are reading right now, you are reading by the Spirit. The word will begin to create in you a dwelling place for the Holy Spirit. You can then invite the Lord in to inhabit your life. Wouldn't you like to just carry Him around wherever you go? David said in Psalm 23:4, "Yea, though I walk through the valley of the shadow of death, I will fear no evil; for You are with me; Your rod and Your staff, they comfort me." He goes on to say in verse 6b, "And I will dwell in the house of the Lord forever."

There can be a perpetual positioning in God where the anointing is always resting upon you. Most of us, at present, tend to come in and out of the anointing quite frequently. Do you know that feeling where you are in the anointing one moment and out the next? But God's will is for us to cross over the barrier. He wants to take us out of the dark place and usher us into the continuous liberty and light of the glory of God where the anointing rests upon us at all times.

Jesus Himself said, "The Spirit of the Lord is upon Me" (Lk. 4:18a), and we know that the Spirit led Him in all of His endeavors. He was even led into the wilderness by the Spirit where He was tempted and tested by satan for forty days and forty nights. But out of that testing period came forth a great resolve in His spirit to do the will of God, and a great anointing came upon

Him. It was after that trial that His ministry was launched upon the earth.

You will find it no different in your life. As you follow the Lord, as the Spirit leads you, you will go through times of testing. First Peter 4:12a says, "Do not think it strange concerning the fiery trial which is to try you." Those testing times that you go through are simply preparation for the victory.

Let's look at the sequence. You must have a will to worship, and once you exercise the will to worship you will be catapulted, or *"harpazo'd"* into the presence of the Lord. To be *harpazo'd* into the presence of the Lord is to be caught up into His presence and to begin to hear the voice of the Lord. Then the hand of God will be upon you.

When you behold the face of God, the hand of God is extended to you. If you look to the hand of God without seeking His face first, you will never find Him. It is when we seek God for who He is that we will find Him. "Looking unto Jesus, the author and finisher of our faith" (Heb. 12:2a).

As we look unto Him without seeking what it is He can do for us, suddenly the Lord's hand will be upon us and He will begin to lead us. We are to continually set our eyes on His face. Christians can be the strangest acting people in town because at times we walk around looking at His face and never stumble or fall because we are keeping our eyes fixed in the right place.

People who worry a lot are always looking around to see what might be sneaking up to attack them. People who are fearful are people who are anxious. But people who have faith keep their eyes in one place, because as you look upon the Lord, then your strength, your substance is drawn from Him.

So the Lord's hand is leading us; and as we worship Him, as we behold the Lord, full of mercy and glory and truth, then that anointing is transferred to us. He leads us through many paths, but all of the paths that we follow are designed for one outcome, and that is to bring us to a place of victory and completion.

A Christian's central focus should be praise. It is when we praise Him that we recognize the anointing and allow His Spirit to become the central focus in our lives. Originally our church was called the "Church on the Rock." We renamed it the "Cathedral of Praise" because the Lord gave us revelation that we have gone through a time in the Body of Christ where there was an emphasis on a form of prayer but now we are emphasizing an attitude of worship.

Prayer is not simply those times when you bend your knee or lie prostrate or stand and recite liturgies. Prayer is really everything you do that is in communion with the Lord. Isaiah 60:18b says, "You shall call your walls Salvation, and your gates Praise." We come into the presence of the Lord through worship.

Our whole focus is to worship the Lord in whatever mode the Lord leads us. Whether it is in silence or speaking corporately, whether with bended knee or standing upright with eyes lifted, it is all a form of prayer; and it ultimately becomes a form of worship to God. We are no longer seeking the Lord for what He can give us. The mark of a true worshiper is a selfless person who has no agenda of what he or she needs.

To worship God with an unselfish heart means that you come to Him without any expectation of your own needs being met. All you come with is an expectation of pleasing Him. If you worship with an agenda of a need to be met, then your worship is clouded by the need. When you worship, you must put all else out of your mind and focus entirely upon Him.

It is when you "Seek first the kingdom of God and His righteousness" that all your needs will be met and "all these thing shall be added to you" (Mt. 6:33). What often hinders corporate worship is when we all come with agendas that we don't leave at the door. To abandon ourselves to the Lord and to be in hot pursuit of Him is awesome.

God is saying that we will be a cathedral of praise. In establishing that, the Lord is doing something very unique in the Church. As I have written, about a year ago we all began to sense that there was anointing resting here, something unspoken or unseen; and we could sense God's presence. We experienced a special manifestation during the time I preached from Hebrews chapter 9 about the tabernacle and the holy place where the ark of the covenant rests.

God's anointing, His presence, and His glory, is in the ark where the Word is, written on tablets of stone. We now have free access into this place where the ark is, where the glory is, where the mercy seat is and where there is forgiveness of sin. Now there is free access to come and hear the voice of God.

Isn't it wonderful that we live in a time that you don't have to go through an intermediary to talk to God? You don't have to go into a little booth, close the window, and confess your sins to a man so that he can confess them to God, and then in turn God can forgive you. You can come boldly to the throne of grace in your time of need. Through the blood of the Lamb, through Jesus Christ, we have access to be redeemed from our sins and have communion with the Father.

We are priests. We can crawl in there and get close to the glory. We don't have to wear bells like the priests under the old covenant did, because through Jesus, the Lord has mercy upon us. The ark is symbolic of what God is putting in your heart. Second Corinthians 3:2 says, "You are our epistle written in our hearts, known and read by all men." God is writing the Word upon our hearts.

If the Word is being written upon our hearts like it was written upon the tablets of stone, and the glory is with the Word, where is the glory at today? It is in you, as Colossians 1:27b says, "Christ in you, the hope of glory."

"But we have this treasure in earthen vessels" (2 Cor. 4:7a), and you are the earthen vessel where the treasure lies. In our church the Lord has emphasized this truth through visible manifestations. These are signs and symbols of that which is taking place within us, for the Kingdom of God is not coming with observation, but is coming from within us. The Kingdom of God is being birthed within a people to be revealed to the earth.

Isaiah 60:1 must come to pass, "Arise, shine; for your light has come! And the glory of the Lord is risen upon you." As this comes to pass there is going to be incredible harvests. For hundreds of years men have tried to find out, How can we bring the harvest?

We have looked at institutions and the plans of man to try to find the best way to market the gospel, but we haven't done a very good job. Obviously people are being saved, but it's usually in spite of us, not because of us, because the Holy Spirit is the one out there doing the work. "The Lord added to the church daily those who were being saved" (Acts 2:47b). We haven't saved anybody, but God is saving multitudes.

What are we to be? We are to be witnesses of His salvation and demonstrate His glory. The world has yet to see the true harvest when people will be born again in such vast numbers that it will be beyond the capability of mankind to reproduce that fast. Amos 9:13 says, " 'Behold, the days are coming,' says the Lord, 'when the plowman shall overtake the reaper, and the treader of grapes him who sows seed; the mountains shall drip with sweet wine, and all the hills shall flow with it.' "

Isaiah 60:1-3 says, "Arise, shine; for your light has come! And the glory of the Lord is risen upon you. For behold, the darkness shall cover the earth, and deep darkness the people; but the Lord will arise over you, and His glory will be seen upon you. The Gentiles shall come to your light, and kings to the brightness of your rising."

As God begins to write His Word upon our hearts, remember it is not just any word; it is the gospel of the Kingdom. He wants to pen the principles of His Word and impregnate them in you so that they become a living Word imparted through you. He desires the nature of Christ to be so revealed in you that no one can deny that His presence abides with you.

You are to become a living epistle to be read and known by all men. When others see you, they will see Him and His glory in you. It doesn't mean you will have a halo around your head or have an aura surround you, even though those things may be evidenced. To be an epistle means that the nature of Christ, the love of God, and the compassion and joy of the Lord will be demonstrated through you. People will see that you have the faith and peace of God.

Wouldn't it be great if we could get to the place that we don't have a fleshly response but rather a divine response to situations round about us? We can rule our circumstances; "And he who rules his spirit [is better] than he who takes a city" (Prov. 16:32b). Through Christ, we can be greater than the things that are trying to oppress us, "because He who is in you is greater than he who is in the world" (1 Jn. 4:4b).

When we are strong in the Lord and in the power of His might, the anointing that rests upon us can break every yoke and liberate every captive. Nothing will be impossible for you if you have faith. You can do exceedingly, abundantly above all that you could ask or think through Christ who strengthens you. You are the soldiers of the Lord, the called, the redeemed of God, and the Lord is establishing His glory in you.

I have asked the Lord, "Why is this cloud coming in our church?" On two occasions we've seen a burst of glory. When the burst of glory came I was amazed; it was so awesome! We were just recalling the burst of glory that had come through the church weeks before, and as I was saying something about the cloud, puff! the glory burst again. It was about three feet long and was shaped like a cylinder. This brightness appeared and then broke into pieces and began to swirl around. It was awesome.

There is an ark that God is establishing in your hearts. There is a cloud of glory resting with us and God is speaking to us. You can get there so quickly too. How long does it take you to get to the throne room? How far away is it? Deuteronomy 30:14a says it is "very near you, in your mouth and in your heart." We can go to the throne room of God anytime we choose. Once you have learned the principal of entering into His presence you will find that it can become automatic. At first you might have to close your eyes and focus, but once you have practiced the pathway to His presence you may get there even with your eyes open.

The Bible talks about rising in the clouds "to meet the Lord in the air" (1 Thess. 4:17b). So many people take this Scripture and try to complicate it and over-spiritualize its simplicity. God cannot speak to the natural man in a spiritual way because the mind of man can't understand. First Corinthians 2:14 says, "But the natural man [cannot comprehend] the things of the Spirit of God, for they are foolishness to him; nor can he know them, because they are spiritually discerned."

But the spiritual man, the one who has his senses trained, can understand the spiritual. The more you come into God's presence, the more your senses become aware of the spiritual realm. It is like when a baby is born and he becomes aware and begins to acquire the ability to walk and to function in his environment. He uses his eyes, his ears, his senses of smell and taste and touch. If you want to get a baby's attention; you speak to him and play with him, and he will then begin to respond.

Imagine putting a baby in an isolated room where you could somehow feed the baby without ever having physical contact. Imagine that he never had contact with anything of this world, with no other human beings. Do you think he would grow up to be normal if all he knew were the four walls that surrounded him?

Many Christians are spiritually in the same boat as that baby because their spiritual man has no perception of how to relate to the Lord. They are related to Him with their senses instead of their spirit. We must become spiritual by making contact with the presence of God. We begin to recognize that it takes awhile and that we are like the baby. It is repeated activity that will create the right responses in us so that we can ultimately achieve the right results.

So you learn how to practice His presence; and once you learn how to get there, it is easy to go there again and again. Have you ever moved to a strange new city and for the first few days and weeks and maybe even months you were lost as a goose? But after awhile you could almost put your car on automatic and get to your destination. I can practically drive to my house blindfolded now because I am so used to the road that leads me home.

It is the same thing in the Spirit. Once you learn to come into God's presence through worship and you break through the veil, it is easier to come back. Each time you return it gets a little easier. Some people make the drive once a week and break through. Then they wait six months before they attempt to drive again and discover that they have forgotten the road to take.

The more you exercise your will to worship, the easier it is to break through each time. Do you want more blessings in your life? The key to having more glory in your life is not to seek more blessings. We should never be blessing seekers. That's a mark of our immaturity. The younger you are in the natural the more you seek to be blessed. The older you get, if you have grown up at all, the more you seek to be a blessing.

The greatest thing that can happen to a young man or a young woman is to have children. There is a transition that takes place in their lives because now they have a responsibility not just to themselves but they are also responsible to take care of and to please someone else. This change should also happen when two people are married. Having someone else to care for takes us out of that self-ish mode and into a giving mode.

In Second Samuel 6, David saw the need to bring the ark of the covenant from the house of Obededom back to its rightful place in Jerusalem. Only the priests could carry the ark while David and the Levites obediently dressed in their fine linen. The glory of the Lord was emanating from the ark and it was causing great joy to come upon those who were bringing it back. The Bible says, "Where the Spirit of the Lord is, there is liberty" (2 Cor. 3:17b).

You may wonder, "Well, I don't know if something is of God or not." It's simple. If it has liberty written all over it, it's of God. If it doesn't have liberty, it's not. "In Your presence is fullness of joy…" (Ps. 16:11b). The greater we experience His presence and the glory, the more joy and liberty we will enjoy.

Some have accused me of being hard on religion. Well, I think man-made religion is just as deadly as the strip club or bar down the road because they all bring people into bondage. Religion limits and confines a person to a legalistic lifestyle that has nothing to do with the life of freedom in Christ. The reason Jesus was crucified was because His middle name was liberty—l-i-b-e-r-t-y.

Jesus was so free that He was willing to heal on the Sabbath. He was so free He was willing to go into the temple, kick out the money changers, and call the place a den of thieves. I wonder how many churches He would visit today with His right foot extended?

He might pay a visit to us, so we better be careful what we say. It is going to rain on the just and the unjust alike. When our obedience is complete, then God stands ready to punish all disobedience. There may still be a little money changing left in our hearts, a little greed, and a little pride. He says get right or get out.

The anointing of the Lord is coming to bring liberty. David had such liberty and joy upon him that he began leaping and dancing and praising the Lord (see 2 Sam. 6). Michal, his wife, was watching her husband, the king, and all the handmaidens were watching too. His wife was from royalty, the daughter of Saul, born into a household full of pride.

As Michal watched her husband leaping and dancing and praising the Lord, she got so upset because she thought David was making a fool out of himself. She said (Bill Hart's translation), "David, you're making a fool out of yourself today in the eyes of the maids and the servants. You're like one of those base fellows, like one of those low-class people that we rule over. Shame, shame, shame, shame."

So David said to Michal, "Woman, I was dancing before God. You listen to me! This was before God and it wasn't before you. God chose me instead of your old man. He put him out of office. He's dead, remember that, he's dead; I'm the king, got it? He put me ruler over the people, over Israel, and so bless God I'm going to play all the music I want to play, as loud as I want to play it, as often as I want to play it, and I'll dance along with it, woman. And I'll even get more undignified now, just because of what you said." Now how many marriages can relate to that?

And guess what happened to Michal? From that day forth she had no children; she became barren and died inside. Spiritual barrenness will happen to you if there is something in you that holds back your worship. If there is something that is restraining you from loving the Lord with all your heart, your mind, and all your strength, then there is a spirit of death on you that is keeping you from bearing fruit. It is preventing you from multiplying the seed that God has planted in you.

Not every personality is going to worship the same way. There are people who are quieter than others and those who are more boisterous, but there is an intensity that must come out of our spirit when the Lord is present and His joy is here, when His glory comes to the house.

I am praying, "Lord, bring the glory so much in our midst that we cannot contain it. Pour out more than we can hold. Let there be a river flow that doesn't just make it to the bottom of our feet, but comes all the way up to where we have to swim in it. Let there be an outpouring of the Holy Spirit that opens flood gates, causes a deluge to come, waters all the dry places, and brings victory everywhere it goes."

Some say, "But I just don't like to praise the Lord that much." But there is glory here and you have got to praise Him! "Well, when I see the glory then I'll praise Him." No, you do it by faith. If you first have faith, then you will have manifestation. If you just let go, He will come. If you just step out there, He'll meet you leaping and dancing and praising the Lord, because the glory is there.

We can find that faith in Acts chapters 1 and 2. The 120 people who gathered on the day of Pentecost were praying in one accord, and all of a sudden this mighty sound came from Heaven. And the place where they were at began to shake, rattle, and roll. Cloven tongues of fire began raining down from Heaven and settled on everybody who was there, and they all began speaking in tongues.

There were people from every nation in Jerusalem celebrating the Passover feast. The people in the crowd began to hear in their own language what was being said. And the multitude wondered how it was possible. Some mocked them and believed they were drunk.

Then Peter stood up and said, "For these are not drunk, as you suppose, since it is only the third hour of the day" (Acts 2:15). And he quoted the prophet Joel, explaining that they were filled with the Holy Spirit. They had been filled with the glory of God!

As they were speaking, everybody there could hear and understand them in their own language. It wasn't that they were all speaking different languages; they were all hearing their own language. How could this happen? Because they just let it go and the Holy Spirit opened the floodgates!

A few years ago, a woman from Vietnam was attending our church one night when I began to speak in tongues from the pulpit. She heard me giving the plan of salvation in her native tongue. A huge impression is made upon a person when he or she hears someone talking in their native language who has never spoken one word of their language before that time. That was the Holy Spirit opening the floodgates in me.

Do you know the glory is with you? Don't go around being a sad sack; get happy and start rejoicing. There is nothing in your life happening that God and you cannot handle together. Just start rejoicing in the Lord. "Rejoice in the Lord always. Again I will say, rejoice!" (Phil. 4:4) Blessed be the Lord.

Glory to God, we love the Lord so much we want to rejoice in His presence! His ark is here, His cloud of glory is here, His voice is here. It's time to rejoice, it's time to be glad, it's time to put off the sackcloth; come out of the ashes and put on a garment of praise to defeat the spirit of heaviness. It's time to rejoice in the Lord! Where the Spirit of the Lord is, there is liberty!

Some people are more demonstrative than others, but I'm asking you to make a conscious effort of your will to do something to bring you through the veil and into the glory. Some may ask, "Why do Christians dance and shout and act like this?" It's because we are a very peculiar people. We understand what Paul meant when he said he became a fool for Christ (see 1 Cor. 4:10).

Do something that brings you out of where you are at right now. For some it might be just putting your hand up in the air. When I first broke through in the Spirit, I was so intimidated by religion that I couldn't even raise my hand above shoulder height. Just try to do something new a little bit at a time.

After awhile you can raise both hands like somebody just made a touchdown! Hallelujah, touchdown Jesus! Just do something to get out of where you are at now. If you're used to dancing, then you may have to run around because you can't just keep on doing what you have done before. Remember Second Corinthians 3:17, "Now the Lord is the Spirit; and where the Spirit of the Lord is, there is liberty."

CHAPTER 7

The Glory Rest

The Lord is continually speaking to my heart about the peace of God. In Isaiah 9:6b-7, Jesus is called the Prince of Peace. It says:

And His name will be called Wonderful, Counselor, Mighty God, Everlasting Father, Prince of Peace. Of the increase of His government and peace there will be no end, upon the throne of David and over His kingdom, to order it and establish it with judgment and justice from that time forward, even forever. The zeal of the Lord of hosts will perform this.

In other words, by His Spirit, it will come to pass; this Word will be in effect. This says that the Lord Jesus has a Kingdom that has no end, established upon the throne and over the Kingdom of David. This Kingdom was built upon the attitude of David's heart, just as the Kingdom that Jesus inherited is built upon His attitude. And you would have to agree, no man has a better attitude than Jesus.

When Jesus walked the earth, nothing interfered with His purpose or attitude. His focus was so pure that He was not deterred in any way from accomplishing His mission. What should speak to us is that we too must realize that our attitude and the position of our hearts determines the ability of our mission to be fulfilled. If we are perverted or crooked in heart, we will fall short of the goals that we have before us.

God honors the pure heart. He dwells in two places, the high and lofty places and in the heart of a contrite man. It is through your humility, brokenness, yieldedness, and the lack of pride in your life that God's holiness is able to inhabit you. You bear witness of this, I am sure, because all of us at one time have "lost it" or "lost our cool" so to speak. We became angry and fell into strife. One always winds up feeling pretty awful in that position. You begin to sense a void of God's Spirit. Before you know it, the flesh begins to consume you.

Jesus comes as the Prince of Peace, bringing rest to His people. There are numerous Scriptures that speak of rest and peace. The definition of resting in the Lord is literally to have peace of mind. The enemy comes to rob, kill, steal, and destroy, to upset your peace of mind and to cause you mental and emotional distress.

Between 1995-96, I made a decision that I was going to walk in peace. At that point I shut off listening to the mouths of those who would try to rob me of peace. Some people think they have a right to speak to you anyway they choose no matter what kind of stress it puts you under. But that's a lie from the devil. You do not have to listen to the accuser of the brethren, and you are under no obligation to tolerate negativity.

You are not birthed into this world with an obligation to be a trash bin where everyone can dump what he or she wants on your head. You can refuse the trash. In New York City, at times the city has had to put their garbage on barges and ship it halfway around the world because their landfills simply would not hold anymore. I tell the devil, "My landfill is closed; you cannot dump your trash on me because I reserve the right to walk in rest and peace." We all have battles and get into conflict, but you choose your battles, when and where. Don't let the enemy make the decisions and impose his will upon you.

When you watch a boxing match, usually you will see that the boxer who makes the initial thrust, or punch, in any exchange, will win the exchange. If a boxer is always defending himself and is not making the initial hit, he will not score as many points as his opponent. We too must not become defensive with the enemy. We can be on the offensive, for Christ came and destroyed the works of the devil. We have been purchased by God and bought with the blood of Jesus, and we have authority in Jesus' name over the principalities and powers of the air.

We have authority in Jesus' name over our minds, our wills, and our emotions. The enemy attempts to destroy our peace of mind and to upset our emotional tranquility, but our rest is in Jesus. The word *rest* is defined as "calm, tranquil, and absence of motion and action." It comes through trusting, depending on, confiding in, putting our hope and refuge in, and finding our retreat, our haven, and our lodging in the Lord.

And so I choose to plant myself in the will of God and not allow myself to become infringed upon by the enemy's whim, because if I can walk in peace, I can walk in victory. Jesus said to the storm, "Peace, be still!" (see Mk. 4:39) With a few words He took command of a raging storm, and we have that same authority in Jesus' name to alter the circumstances of life, through faith in His power.

We might not change all the circumstances around us, but we can alter the atmosphere. We can become isles of tranquility in the midst of the storm. We can be peacemakers. The Bible says, "Let us pursue the things which make for peace" (Rom. 14:19a). A peacemaker is able to go to where there is conflict and bring resolution. If two people are fighting, you can step in the middle. You have to step carefully because you might get hit, but you can speak to them and bring peace and resolution to the conflict.

Peace and rest are synonymous. In the Book of Isaiah, Jesus is called the Prince of Peace. Jesus said in Matthew 11:29, "Take My yoke upon you and learn from Me, for I am gentle and lowly in heart, and you will find rest for your souls." Jesus is the one who comes into our lives to give us rest and peace and takes our yoke upon Him. We can turn all our burdens over to the Lord for He cares for us. There remains a rest for the people of God.

Look at the following verses from the Bible and see God's wonderful promises to His people.

> *Peace I leave with you, My peace I give to you; not as the world gives do I give to you. Let not your heart be troubled, neither let it be afraid* (John 14:27).

> *The Lord will give strength to His people; the Lord will bless His people with peace* (Psalm 29:11).

> *I will both lie down in peace, and sleep; for You alone, O Lord, make me dwell in safety* (Psalm 4:8).

> *Great peace have those who love Your law, and nothing causes them to stumble* (Psalm 119:165).

> *When you lie down, you will not be afraid; yes, you will lie down and your sleep will be sweet* (Proverbs 3:24).

Have you ever had a battle while you slept? I have fought the hordes of hell in my dreams, and I kind of like that because the outcome of that battle is victory. I am battling through to find peace.

> *For to be carnally minded is death, but to be spiritually minded is life and peace* (Romans 8:6).

> *Be anxious for nothing, but in everything by prayer and supplication, with thanksgiving, let your requests be made known to God; and the peace of God, which surpasses all understanding, will guard your hearts and minds through Christ Jesus* (Philippians 4:6-7).

> *Now may the Lord of peace Himself give you peace always in every way. The Lord be with you all* (2 Thessalonians 3:16).

> *My lips shall greatly rejoice when I sing to You, and my soul, which you have redeemed* (Psalm 71:23).

Genesis 2:2b says, "And He [God] rested on the seventh day...." The significance of the seventh day is what we commonly acknowledge as the Day of the Kingdom. This is the day when the lion will lie down with the lamb and swords will be turned into plowshares. We live on battlefield earth, but battlefield earth is going to turn into Kingdom peace.

God will bring true restoration to the earth, and what He is restoring is His presence. When Adam and Eve were in the garden they were not alone; God was there with them. I do not know if He was there in physical form, but He spoke to them as audibly as I speak to you. He was there in spirit and they were acutely aware of His presence.

The garden of Eden was overshadowed with the glory of God because Eden was the place of creation that God birthed out of His glory. It is only in the presence of the Lord or the manifestation of God that true creation can take place. Jesus says in John 3:5b, "Unless one is born of water and the Spirit, he cannot enter the kingdom of God."

You show me someone who says they are born again but never has sensed God in a mighty way, and I will show you someone who has made a mental assent to salvation but has not yet had a true spiritual conversion. For someone to profess "I'm born again," with no radical change in their life is someone who is deceived. True faith that creates salvation will always carry such an anointing that it follows with a radical transformation.

You do not have to convince people to walk with God if they have truly met Him. If we have to try to persuade people through human efforts to accept the things of God then we have done them a disservice because they are not yet born again.

When you are born again, your eyes will be opened and your ears will begin to hear the Spirit of God speaking to you. You will not need anyone to prod you to get involved in a discipleship class. You will not need anyone to call you on Sunday morning and make sure you are going to be in church. I think Billy Graham has done a most awesome work on the earth, but I think he would be the first to admit that many of the hordes of people who walk the aisle at the crusades cannot be found afterwards attending any church. Have they truly been born again? If there is not a radical change in their life, one must wonder.

The anointing will always bring radical change in your life, and you cannot be born again apart from the anointing. Unless the Spirit of God is hovering over you, there can be no creation in you. Second Corinthians 5:17 says, "If anyone is in Christ, he is a new creation...." The moment we are new creations in Christ we are motivated to serve the Lord. It goes on to say, "...old things have passed away; behold, all things have become new."

Conversion is a fantastic experience, but a mental assent to conversion only brings confusion. It brings a false hope and a false promise without the reality of transformation.

The Lord rested on the seventh day from His work of creation, and His glory hovered over that which He created. One doesn't give birth to life and then just abandon it. What God births He also equips. You were conceived by the Holy Spirit, and He equips you by His Spirit to fulfill that which He has destined for you to become.

When Adam and Eve fell from grace because of their sin, they separated themselves from the life-changing Spirit, the anointing that would maintain and keep them moving ahead in the will of God. They cut themselves off from God's Spirit, and when they did so they suddenly had a revelation of their nakedness and shame that goes far beyond just the physical.

All of a sudden they were barren of the glory, for the glory was their covering. It remained that way until 2000 years ago when Jesus Christ was born in Bethlehem of a virgin in the manger. He lived the example of a perfect Son, giving His life for us on the cross as the Son of God.

At that moment, when Christ died on the cross, the Spirit of the Lord returned to the earth. There was an unprecedented conversion that took place among the apostles and disciples during the time between the crucifixion and the resurrection. We see that the transition continued as we read the account written in the Book of Acts. Jesus' followers were cowering and afraid and had no revelation of what was going on whatsoever because they had not yet received the promise of the Holy Spirit.

But after the resurrection, after the Spirit of the Lord came on the day of Pentecost, from that moment forth they experienced a radical transformation. Those fearful, timid, cowardly disciples and apostles became the mighty men and women of God who turned the world upside down! They were made strong and bold by the anointing because from that moment forth the glory overshadowed their every action, their every move.

The apostles and disciples had moved into the realm where the Lord said we could become co-creators and joint heirs with Him. They had the same Spirit upon them that Jesus possessed. Not since the garden of Eden could men step forward with such boldness and live in such absolute victory.

The great men of faith such as Abraham, Isaac, Jacob, Moses, and David lived in mighty victory too, but they could not enjoy what we do today. They did not have the presence of the Lord continually abiding with them. Even Moses would have to go to the tent of meeting to experience God's anointing and hope that the time he spent there would sustain him for the times when he was absent from the Lord.

But now we can consistently and continually walk into the tent of meeting. We have the ability to abide in the anointing and bask in the glory cloud. God is restoring His Kingdom in our midst. The more that we open ourselves to be filled with the Spirit, the more we will see restoration come.

Even though I am not a big believer in medicine, I would like you to look at the following example. If you put an IV with antibiotic into someone, it will flow into their system and bring about some cure. If you put in a little bit more, it will bring even more of a cure. It is the same with the Spirit—the more we open up, the more we will receive. We will gain more insight, revelation, wisdom, authority, power, boldness, confidence, and strength; and we will begin to walk in greater peace.

The absence of peace is simply the absence of the anointing. The absence of joy is the absence of the anointing. A lack of anointing in the mind of man will ultimately be replaced with confusion. The more we sow to the flesh the more confusion we walk in. The more we are in the Spirit, the more of a sound mind we begin to possess. We then can lock into a vision that cannot be deterred by any obstacles we may face.

As the anointing magnifies in the days ahead, we will have no need of psychiatrists or psychoanalysis; we will only have need for more glory. These thoughts may sound idealistic but I like being an idealist because I believe that the Lord wants us to preach an ideal existence.

But what keeps us away from the glory and the anointing? There are three kinds of works we see in the Bible. There are "wicked works" that originate from a fallen condition. Works that have the same fruit and the same origin as satan's spirit are called wicked works. Rotten fruit originates from an unrepentant, unregenerate heart. Out of this heart spews forth bitterness and rebellion.

Christians can bring forth wicked works. I have far more concern about Christian witchcraft than I do about witchcraft in the covens. Christian witchcraft originates out of those who have let their hearts become bitter because of a lack of repentance. They might have started out in the Lord, and they might have been experiencing the grace and the mercy of God, but somewhere they shut off the flow of forgiveness.

If Christians cannot receive forgiveness, they are not able to give it. If you do not have an understanding of the awesome forgiveness of the Lord, then you will have no room in your heart to forgive anyone else. It is only in your personal knowledge of God that you are able to convey God to anyone else. It is only as you have been forgiven that you are able to forgive. If you do not know what it is like to be forgiven, you will not be able to forgive others.

Christian witchcraft and wicked works begin out of the fallen nature of man and out of an unrepentant heart. This is a heart that has become bitter because of rejection, repetitive disobedience to God, and consistent unwillingness to forgive those who have hurt you. This becomes a wicked heart. As Hebrews 12:15 says, "Looking carefully lest anyone fall short of the grace of God; lest any root of bitterness springing up cause trouble, and by this many become defiled."

Witchcraft can spring up out of the human soul; it is a vile thing that literally charges the spirit realm and curses the things around it. Wicked people tend to want to associate with those of like spirit.

Once as I was driving my Harley-Davidson motorcycle and passed a biker bar, I noticed a row of Harley-Davidson's lined up out front, but I was not even tempted to stop. I did not belong in that place, and if I would have gone in there, I would have felt like a square peg in a round hole. I would not have fit in even though there were other Harley riders in there.

Why? Those bikers were there because they were attracted to one another's way of life, and so they flock together. You would not find those same Harley's parked in front of our church and gathered together with us on a Sunday morning. Hopefully, someday that will happen, but for now many are gathered at the biker bar as one. They seek out others who live the same lifestyle, believing that the power they possess comes in their numbers. But they are deceived, because they do not realize that they are living in a continual place of defeat.

When Christians continually live in a place of defeat, they will try to find others who also live in the same defeat. Often times your success at any endeavor will depend entirely on those you associate with. You will not keep bad company if you have good intentions, nor will you associate with murmurers, complainers, or bitter people if you have any desire to be a part of the Kingdom.

The Bible says that murmurers, complainers, liars, cheaters, and people who are unrepentant will have no place in the Kingdom. The Kingdom is closed to them (see Eph. 5:5 and 1 Cor. 6:10.)

You may ask, "Oh, do you mean they're not saved; they're not going to Heaven?" No, they might be saved and go to Heaven, but they will not ever partake of the Kingdom here on earth. The Kingdom of God is a lifestyle of righteousness, peace, and joy in the Holy Spirit. As Christians living in the Kingdom, we offer a lifestyle that is awesome with victory after victory. Triumphant victory and overcoming is our way of life where wicked works are given no place.

"Dead works" is the second type of works that originate from a religious spirit; they have no life-giving qualities. Dead works are works that we feel compelled to do out of constraint or obligation. We do these works thinking, Well, I've got to go through the motions because I must do what I've always been told good Christians are supposed to do, and I want to make a good impression.

Of course, if you are working for someone, you should do what they tell you to do. But by and large in your life, the older and wiser you get, the more you will learn to do only those things that are profitable. We do not have time to waste on things that are not profitable for the Kingdom.

"Good works" originate from the Spirit and are works that remain. My grandmother exemplified the true meaning of good works. My grandmother's home had only one heater in the little living room; there was no heat in the two bedrooms. When we were little kids, we would sometimes stay with her in the wintertime; and after taking our baths, we'd run to the bedroom and jump under her huge thick covers, quilts, and blankets, which would envelop us. I loved it!

It felt so cold when we would first jump in, but it did not take long to start getting toasty-warm. It was so comfortable; it felt like you were back in your mother's womb. If you haven't had a chance to enjoy that, I would encourage you to turn off all the heat in your house, grab some thick covers, and crawl in. It's heaven on earth.

My little grandmother passed away in 1972 when she was 88 years old. She had a saying on the wall, "Only one life 'twill soon be past; only what's done for Christ will last." Those were the "good works," the things that are produced by the Spirit. I believe that only the selfless acts that are done for Christ will last. Only those things will bring peace.

> *There remains therefore a rest for the people of God. For he who has entered His rest has himself also ceased from his works as God did from His. Let us therefore be diligent to enter that rest, lest anyone fall according to the same example of disobedience. For the word of God is living and powerful, and sharper than any two-edged sword, piercing even to the division of soul and spirit, and of joints and marrow, and is a discerner of the thoughts and intents of the heart. And there is no creature hidden from His sight, but all things are naked and open to the eyes of Him to whom we must give account* (Hebrews 4:9-13).

Let's be diligent to go into the place that God has reserved for His people, for "there remains therefore a rest for the people of the Lord" (v. 9). Religious activity is no substitute for a calm spirit, peace, joy, and the place of abiding in Him. John tells us that we are to abide in the Lord, and as we do, whatever we ask of Him in His name, it shall be done (see Jn. 14:12-14). That's learning to rest in the Lord.

True faith has no futility—no grunt power attached to it. Even though sometimes our emotions will cause us to shout and scream and holler, true faith has no emotion. It is a position, a rest. If you really believe God, trust Him and stand on the promise. No matter what comes, never take your eyes off the promise.

Winds, storms, affliction, trials, accusers, and persecution may come, but all the while you can be calm in the midst of the storm because you know that Jesus is with you and nothing can destroy you. You step into rest, and out of fear, futility, anxiety, and frustration. These are of satan's spirit, not of the Lord's. Satan's nature is to always press you to make a quick decision and do something out of character in a moment of trial.

When a trial comes and the battle rages on, that is the time to make sure that you do not make any quick decisions. Never make a life-changing decision in the midst of a battle because you will be stepping out of the place of protection and opening up yourself for an onslaught that you will not be able to stand against. In the flesh we are no match for the enemy. He mops you up if you try to fight him in the flesh.

Look at the world in general. Right now it is estimated that there are over 200 million people in the world who are in transit, displaced by wars, pestilence, and famine. Two hundred million people are living like nomads right now in many countries. Never before in the history of humanity has there been such massive displacement. And a large amount of this population is in one of the stages of AIDS, which will eventually kill them.

These devastating circumstances represent the spirit of the devil because he is out to kill, steal, and destroy all of mankind. We still have the protection that we embrace in America only because we have a core of people who have put their trust in Christ and believe in God. But countries that practice satanic religions and worship false gods are wide open to his destruction. There is no immunity, and to satan, they have simply become flesh that he can massacre and destroy at will. It's awful what the devil is doing to humanity around the world.

The only hope for the people of this earth is Jesus Christ. The battle is so intense that if the Lord hadn't shortened the days all flesh would be destroyed. That is how determined the enemy is, to destroy the creation of God and the people of the Lord. But it is only in the remnant that salvation will be found. It is only in those who have a revelation of their awesome authority and stature before God that salvation will be found upon the earth.

You are the hope of the glory of God and of all creation. Romans 8:19 says, "For the earnest expectation of the creation eagerly waits for the revealing of the sons of God." In the last days the sons of God will have such authority that they will be able to go into a nation of chaos and stop the enemy's hand. They will rebuke the devourer and protect the massive hordes of humanity that are even now being destroyed by the enemy.

The Muslims and Hindus and others of the world who worship false gods may be fine people with good intentions, but they are not worshiping the one true God and therefore have no immunity from the powers of the devil. But one day they will see the Son of God revealed unto them; and multitudes will turn their hearts to God, bow their knees to Jesus Christ, and confess Him as Lord.

Satan with his great wrath has been unleashed upon the earth. He is out to destroy all the people of the earth. I do not know what God's timetable is, but we could very well be in the beginning stages of the tribulation. Maybe you thought you would be raptured before it all started. But you shouldn't want to get out of here. You should want to stay because you point the way to the answer. During the days of trial, God will use you to bring many to Christ. It will not be pleasant to be here, but you will be rewarded greatly for enduring to the end.

Tell everybody else they can go, but you will stay because you are going to fight the good fight of faith. A great warrior never retreats in the day of battle but stands and fights knowing that because he has a just cause he will win the victory. Generals Patton, McArthur, Eisenhower, and Bradley may have been great generals and great warriors, but they are nothing compared to our General, Jesus Christ.

Once our hearts are right, we cease from our labor and strife. The attitudes of the Kingdom that we begin to move into are so awesome! We begin to absolutely trust in God. We learn to roll our cares upon Him, learning to lean, not upon our own understanding and wisdom, but upon the arm of the great I Am. He who is in me is greater than the one who is within the world. He is my strength, my refuge, my fortress, my high tower. He is my peace, my joy, my hope and strength. This Savior who came as the Prince of Peace has come to give me peace in my heart. "But those who wait on the Lord shall renew their strength; they shall mount up with wings like eagles, they shall run and not be weary, they shall walk and not faint" (Isaiah 40:31).

When we walk in the soul, the voice of our Father grows dim. When we walk in the flesh, the presence of the Lord seems far away and we wind up in an unending maze of confusion.

At times in my life I have felt like I am in one of those mazes in which rats are placed and can't get out. I have felt like I was bumping off one wall and into another. It is only when I turn back to the Spirit that I find my direction because He becomes like a lamp unto my feet. He becomes an anchor to my soul and brings me out of the place of frustration and futility. He breaks the chains of bondage that have been holding me back, and He renews and restores my soul. My confidence is strong in Him, and I become strong in the Lord and in the power of His might.

To achieve this strength we must once again seek the right path. Every time you get off the path, quickly find it again and get back on track. The flesh is so treacherous and deceitful that it only takes a moment, the blink of an eye to lose your way.

But thank God it only takes another moment to get back on His path. Even when you find yourself falling off into the abyss of darkness, all you have to do is call unto Him and He will hear you and will answer.

> *Behold, the Lord's hand is not shortened, that it cannot save; nor His ear heavy, that it cannot hear. But your iniquities have separated you from your God; and your sins have hidden His face from you, so that He will not hear (Isaiah 59:1-2).*

When we find that separation from God is taking place because of something that we have done, either inadvertently or willfully, we need to simply cry out and extend our hand from out of the pit and say, "Lord, bring me out of this place. Oh God, set me on a high hill that I may see again. Open my ears that I may hear what the Spirit of the Lord would say to the Church."

When His voice becomes dim and no guidance is provided, we wind up in a chain of bondage, confusion, and frustration. We must come back to the Lord and say, "Lord, lead us in paths of righteousness for Thy name's sake! Lead us in the place of rest and victory! Let us go to the place of joy that Christ had where, for the joy set before Him, He was able to endure even the cross. Lord, we don't have to go through the same cross that You went through, but let us have such a vision of You before us while we endure what we are going through. Let us know that joy unspeakable and full of glory rules our hearts!" And the peace of God will guard our hearts and rule our minds.

We learn to lean upon the I Am so that we may know that He is, and that He is a rewarder of them who diligently seek Him. For He is the Great I Am, the ever present, omnipresent God, always here with His Spirit, hovering like a mother hen over her chicks, calling us to come and follow Him. Follow Him. He will lead us as soul winners into fruitfulness. He will lead us into greener pastures and enable us to become what He has called us to be, according to His good will and purposes.

CHAPTER 8

He Is Glory

The Lord is speaking to us and saying that every aspect of our life centers on the glory. God wants to bring us into the place where there is a continual manifestation of His presence in every area of our life. The presence of the Lord is so important that Moses said in Exodus 33:15, "If Your Presence does not go with us, do not bring us up from here." His presence comes because we have sought His face and we do it so, as Paul said in Philippians 3:10, "That I may know Him and the power of His resurrection, and the fellowship of His sufferings, being conformed to His death."

Christ came and gave everything to us. He gave His life as a ransom for all men. This was the ultimate price that had to be paid to bring freedom to the hostages. We were held hostage, in bondage and trapped in sin. Our ransom giver willingly said, "I will step in their place and will substitute Myself for them, so they won't have to pay that price." And what was the price? Death. Because, as Paul writes, "For the wages of sin is death, but the gift of God is eternal life in Christ Jesus our Lord" (Rom. 6:23).

One of the beautiful things about knowing the Lord is understanding what He gave us. I have often thought about what I could accomplish in this life if I could only approach just a small measure of the nature of Christ and the way that He gave. If I could do that, I could live a meaningful life and leave a significant impact upon this world.

A word came to me from a dear brother that God was going to raise up a Joseph company, and he saw that on my life the Lord was placing the ring and the robe of a Joseph ministry. It really has begun to sink into my heart that my church has become a Joseph company, a people who give. The Lord says that the number of people in our church is insignificant, because it is not how many, but how much the how many give.

Even churches with large numbers can have little impact if they give little. In Judges 7 we see Gideon's army of only 300 men and how they became a mighty force to be reckoned with. The Lord can take that which seems small in the eyes of men and make something great in the Kingdom.

What is in your hand? What has God given you that can make a significant difference in the age that we live in? What God has given you can make a monumental impact. Your gift can become massive and awesome if the Spirit of the Lord is upon it, because the Spirit of the Lord is a spirit of generosity and love.

Genesis 2 says that the Lord created the heavens and the earth; He created all the beasts of the field, the fowl of the air, the fish in the sea; He created man and woman, Adam and Eve; and He created a place where they lived called the garden. And on the seventh day the Lord rested.

When God rested, He ceased from His labor. He worked and accomplished all that He intended and then rested and called that day the Sabbath. The Sabbath day is when we come and reflect upon that which has been accomplished during the previous six days.

Many biblical scholars believe that the seventh day represents the day of the Kingdom. During that time man will strive for six days and on the seventh day the lamb will lie down with the lion and those at war will beat their weapons into plowshares. It will be a day of peace upon the earth. During this thousand years, Revelation 20:2 says that satan will no longer be able to release his fury, his deception, and his hatred onto humanity.

We know that we as a people are anticipating the day of the Kingdom. We are anticipating the day when there is no evil upon the earth, a glorious reign when there will be no deception, death, tears or fear, only the presence of the Lord Himself. When Jesus came, He said, "Surely the kingdom of God has come upon you" (Lk. 11:20b). He was referring to Himself because Jesus is the Kingdom. When we seek the Kingdom, we are actually seeking the King. If we can get the King on the scene, we have got the Kingdom in our midst.

So we ask the Lord Jesus to come because "Thy kingdom come" is who He is. His very presence brings everything that we are seeking. His presence brings peace, joy, righteousness, and freedom from fear.

So the seventh day is the day of the Kingdom when the Lord rested. We too observe the Sabbath, and we observe it on Sunday. Under the old covenant the Sabbath day was Saturday, but the law ceases to bind us. We are now under grace and no longer obligated to observe the exact days and seasons of the old covenant to be in the Spirit. Thank God for that.

But there is still a special significance to the Sabbath. It is a day where we come and commune more intensely than any other day. It is a day that we reserve for reflection, rest, recuperation, restoration; and it is a day that we come and give blessings and thankfulness for that which the Lord has given us. And we have a lot to be thankful for. Psalm 118:24 says, "This is the day the Lord has made; we will rejoice and be glad in it." In Isaiah chapter 9 we see these beautiful verses:

> *Nevertheless the gloom will not be upon her who is distressed, as when at first He lightly esteemed the land of Zebulun and the land of Naphtali, and afterward more heavily oppressed her, by the way of the sea, beyond the Jordan, in Galilee of the Gentiles. The people who walked in darkness have seen a great light; those who dwelt in the land of the shadow of death, upon them a light has shined* (Isaiah 9:1-2).

Isaiah the prophet is prophesying about the coming of the Lord. In my opinion Isaiah should be the premier Book of the Old Testament because the prophet not only foretells the coming of Jesus, but he also foretells the coming of the Kingdom and details this establishment of God upon the earth. Nowhere else do we find a more explicit depiction of the nature of Christ than in the Book of Isaiah.

In Isaiah 61:1, we see the prophecy that Jesus Himself quoted in Luke 4:18-19. Jesus said,

> *The Spirit of the Lord is upon Me, because He has anointed Me to preach the gospel to the poor; He has sent Me to heal the brokenhearted, to proclaim liberty to the captives and recovery of sight to the blind, to set at liberty those who are oppressed; to proclaim the acceptable year of the Lord* (Luke 4:18-19).

And Isaiah 61 goes on to say in verses 2b-3,

> *And the day of vengeance of our God; to comfort all who mourn, to console those who mourn in Zion, to give them beauty for ashes, the oil of joy for mourning, the garment of praise for the spirit of heaviness; that they may be called trees of righteousness, the planting of the Lord, that He may be glorified.*

This prophecy about Jesus told of One who would come with great anointing, able to break the yokes and put to naught the works of the devil. The One foretold of would begin to establish His people and show them the way to the Father. It goes on to talk about what will happen as God brings this ministry to these people and liberates them.

It says in Isaiah 61:4-7:

> *And they shall rebuild the old ruins, they shall raise up the former desolations, and they shall repair the ruined cities, the desolations of many generations.*

Strangers shall stand and feed your flocks, and the sons of the foreigner shall be your plowmen and your vinedressers. But you shall be named the priests of the Lord, they shall call you the servants of our God. You shall eat the riches of the Gentiles, and in their glory you shall boast. Instead of your shame you shall have double honor, and instead of confusion they shall rejoice in their portion. Therefore in their land they shall possess double; everlasting joy shall be theirs (Isaiah 61:4-7).

This Scripture reflects upon the very group of people who were in prison, who were mourning, who were poor and in a place of heaviness. They were oppressed, depressed, and beaten up. This same group of people are the ones who will reveal the ancient ruins, rebuild all that is to be restored and will be called priests of God and servants of God. They will eat the riches of the Gentiles, possess double honor instead of confusion, and they will have everlasting joy upon them.

Wherever you are at, if you will allow the anointing to break the yoke, you can become a mighty overcomer. Daniel said, "The people who know their God shall be strong, and carry out great exploits" (Dan. 11:32b). Who are those people who will do these things? It will not be the mighty or the proud, and it will not be those who seemingly have their act together.

The greatest preachers and the greatest prophets in the last days will not be those who have been educated by men, but they will be those who have been so blessed of God that the anointing of the Lord will be upon them. What you know is not important; it is Who you know. It is not how much your mind has comprehended, but it is how many chains have been broken off you. It is not the amount of knowledge you have obtained in the eyes of men, but how deep a pit you have been dug out of that will cause you to have influence upon the earth.

The grace that God gives us will not be nullified nor will it be for naught. God's grace will be magnified through us. Jesus was called a seed, a grain. He said in John 12:24, "Unless a grain of wheat falls into the ground and dies, it remains alone; but if it dies, it produces much grain." You are also God's seed, and the Lord wants to take you and bear much fruit through you.

Jesus died, was buried, and on the third day was raised again to walk in newness of life. He lived and walked among the disciples in a glorified state, then ascended to the throne at the right hand of the Father where He ever lives to make intercession for us. He has prepared a place for us where we too can be seated with Him in heavenly places with the heavenly Father.

We are joint heirs with Christ in every respect. He has written us into His will and testament and brought us into a place of inheritance, authority, anointing, and wisdom beyond what the mind can fathom. "Eye has not seen, nor ear heard, nor have entered into the heart of man the things which God has prepared for those who love Him" (1 Cor. 2:9).

Christ came to loose us into His glorious liberty. Second Corinthians 3:17 says, "Now the Lord is the Spirit; and where the Spirit of the Lord is, there is liberty." And in Matthew 4:16, "The people who sat in darkness have seen a great light, and upon those who sat in the region and shadow of death light has dawned."

Jesus said in Matthew 5:14a, "You are the light of the world." The light is shining from Him into us, and we become the light and salt of the whole earth. If we are the light of the world, let's not hide this light under a basket. Let's take off the basket and let it shine; let it be revealed.

I had an awesome dream. I was walking through the glory cloud, which was very thick, and suddenly the cloud began to adhere to my skin. I remember walking into the church with glory all over me. One of our church members, Jack, was looking at it and rubbing it. The glory was thick and falling off me, and a white substance was covering my shoes. Jack was astonished and said, "Wow, look at that!" And I said, "Yeah, Jack, the glory is coming down now, and we're walking through it and it's covering us."

We were getting excited. Even though Jack and I are "long in the tooth," we were acting like children, rejoicing in His presence. Sometimes I would like to take some of the young people and say, "Hey, refocus yourself a little bit here; what's important is what's happening in the Spirit."

It is so easy to forget our purpose, but we have been called to be the light of the world and the salt of the earth. These are truly the days of Elijah, where God is restoring to the Church a new mantle of glory. A new anointing is coming, the profound authority of the Word. Think about this: The Word of the Lord is going to be like eating a delectable meal. It is going to become so delicious, so sweet and delightful. What Jesus said in Matthew 4:4b will become a special reality for His people: "Man shall not live by bread alone, but by every word that proceeds from the mouth of God."

I used to wonder what that Scripture meant. How can man live by the Word of God and not by bread? Most of what I heard of the Word of God was some sermonizing and theology or shouting and screaming, and who wanted to eat that? You become what you eat. If you have an angry preacher, you will have a lot of angry people. If you have a judgmental preacher, you will have a lot of judgmental people. If you have a sound mind and your heart's desire is to feed on the Word, then you will become what God intended you to be.

> *You have multiplied the nation and increased its joy; they rejoice before You according to the joy of harvest, as men rejoice when they divide the spoil. For You have broken the yoke of his burden and the staff of his shoulder, the rod of his oppressor, as in the day of Midian....For unto us a Child is born, unto us a Son is given; and the government will be upon His shoulder. And His name will be called Wonderful,*

Counselor, Mighty God, Everlasting Father, Prince of Peace (Isaiah 9:3-4,6).

In these verses we see a child, a son, and finally a father. In life, each has a different function and responsibility.

Is Jesus still a lamb? Is He still a Son? Is He still a Father? Do we need all of these? Yes! First, we need Him as a lamb so that He could be sacrificed and offered up in our place. Secondly, we need Him as a son of obedience who learned perfect submission through His sufferings. And like Christ, we also learn to submit through trials we face and the sufferings we endure. And lastly, we need Him as a father because as we mature in Him, we are responsible to carry the message of glory to all the children of the world. In every way we follow Him as the pattern.

Romans 8:29b says, "He might be the firstborn among many brethren." We are the brethren (or sons) who God is birthing into a new level of son-ship. He is raising us to become manifested sons, which means a completed son, one who now has the authority of the Father fully vested upon him. But some of us do not become completed sons; we remain as babes.

A baby in the Lord knows Jesus as Savior and nothing more. He walks around all the time saying, "Mama, change my diaper! I'm hungry, I'm cold, I'm hot, I'm lonely, I'm fearful, I'm hurting; I need somebody to help me!" He carries a big sign that says, "I need something!" You feed him, but within three hours he is hungry again. You change his diaper, but three hours later it is dirty again, and you think, Where does all this stuff come from?

It is God's will that each of us grows up to be a son who can take care of the basic things for himself. A son can then become a father. When he takes on a father's role, he then moves into a whole different realm. He is then in a place of authority and a place where he can charter his destiny, not only for himself but also that of others.

Jesus came as a little child-lamb, became a Son, ascended to the right hand of the Father, and He said in John 17:22, "The glory which You gave Me I have given them, that they may be one just as We are one." This means we can share the same glory, the same mission, the same purpose, words, thoughts, and intentions. We can have the same goals and become one in everything.

The Lord is saying that the revelation you have of Him will determine the stature that you have in Him. If your revelation is based only on your needs and you come to the Lord only for the basics, then you will always be in a shallow relationship with Him. When you come to realize that you do not have to keep asking over and over again for God's provision, you then will become a son who experiences a deeper and more intimate walk with the Father.

That's great, but there is one step further that we must take. The Holy Spirit wants to reveal to you the wisdom of the Father so that you can become like Him. As Jesus said in Matthew 5:48, "Therefore you shall be perfect, just as your Father in heaven is perfect." What you and I can believe for and experience today is the ability to walk in the nature of God while we are here upon the earth just as Christ Himself did. We can challenge ourselves and begin to confess the following:

"I'm going to walk in the authority of God upon the earth and no longer will I ever look to Him to say, 'Lord, I've got a need'; but I'll always look and say, 'Where is the need that I can meet?' It is time I raised some babes into sons. Paul wrote in First Corinthians 13:11, 'When I was a child, I spoke as a child...but when I became a man, I put away childish things.' Now it's my turn to assume the responsibility to meet the needs of the children."

Does it mean that we are to have a church full of fathers and no children? No. We should be a church that is continually birthing babies. If we are not reproducing, it is because we are not taking on the father's role. We are still behaving immaturely and not assuming responsibility. The Lord wants you to assume the responsibility.

You are to go out and multiply and bring forth some babies. I know they are a mess. They cry and require constant attention, but your greatest responsibility is to meet others' needs. If you do not start meeting needs, then you will die spiritually. You will not be worth anything. You will not be useful to God unless you start learning to give as the Father gave to us. It is when you begin to give more than you are trying to receive that you demonstrate proof that the mark of the Father is on you.

> *Of the increase of His government and peace there will be no end. Upon the throne of David and over his kingdom, to order it and establish it with judgment and justice from that time forward, even forever. The zeal of the Lord of hosts will perform this* (Isaiah 9:7).

The Lord desires to bring His peace to you—peace of mind, mental and emotional. He entreats you to depend and trust in Him to bring you into a tranquil, calm existence. The Father wants you to roll your cares upon Him, for He cares for your soul.

Worry and unrest is a work of the flesh. When we are in distress, it is evidence that the flesh is hard at work. This is the time for communion with God, through worship and a holy devotion to Him. This is a time for the Church to devote our hearts to a higher place in the Lord and to worship and adore Him.

We bring a sacrifice of praise to God and in return we are rewarded with the peace of God that passes all understanding. We bring our hearts as a sacrifice to the Lord, and in return we are offered rest from our labors. We learn to lean upon Him, because He is the I Am.

In Exodus 3:13-14, as Moses was before the burning bush, talking to God, he asked,

*"Indeed, when I come to the children of Israel and say
to them, 'The God of your fathers has sent me to you,'
and they say to me, 'What is His name?' what shall I
say to them?" And God said to Moses, "I AM WHO I
AM." And He said, "Thus you shall say to the children
of Israel, 'I AM has sent me to you.'"*

So we ask, "Who are You, God?" And He answers, "I Am." "But what does that mean?" "I Am." "And Lord, how do I interpret that?" "I Am." And you keep wondering, Why does He keep saying, "I Am"? What does this mean? You argue with it and try to figure it out, and then you understand and can finally say, "He Is."

If God keeps saying to you, "I Am" long enough, finally one day you will say, "He Is." He is the author of your salvation. He is the rock and your refuge. He is your eternal weight of glory. He is the peace that passes all understanding. He is your authority and the One you lean upon and trust. He is the One you run to in time of need. He is the One who will reward them that diligently seek Him. He is the One who will appear in your midst. He is the One who will reveal His glory into His people. He is the One, hallelujah!

CHAPTER 9

Glory Evangelism

With the presence and manifestations of the Lord that God is bringing into our midst and throughout the world today, evangelism as we have known it will cease to exist. When you read the Book of Acts you learn that their evangelism was empowered by the Holy Spirit. The Spirit of God sent them forth with great power and authority. As Acts 5:15 says, "They brought the sick out into the streets and laid them on beds and couches, that at least the shadow of Peter passing by might fall on some of them." Now that's waves of glory!

Many of today's churches, because of their lack of power and anointing, have reverted to alternative methods of evangelism. It is not that those methods are necessarily wrong, but God's perfect plan is for people to be reborn in the presence of the Lord. When the Holy Spirit is present, He will anoint you with power on high just as He did for those on the day of Pentecost. What you are born into is usually a determining factor of who and what you become.

We are more of a product of our environment and upbringing than of our race or any other factor that might influence us. The same holds true for our spiritual life. That is why if one is raised in a legalistic environment, it is difficult for them to step out in blind faith and enter into the Kingdom of glory.

People who are born into households that teach righteousness comes only through the law, find it extremely hard to accept grace through faith. They have been taught from early childhood that their right standing with God comes from good works and deeds, which creates an open door for the spirit of legalism to plant itself firmly in their belief system. Galatians 5:4 says, "You have become estranged from Christ, you who attempt to be justified by law; you have fallen from grace."

In Luke 14:16-24, Jesus told a parable of a rich man who invited people to a great banquet. But when it came time for the banquet, they all gave excuses as to why they couldn't come. The rich man got angry, and he rose up and told his servant, "Go out quickly into the streets and lanes of the city, and bring in the poor and the maimed and the lame and the blind."

And so it will be in the last days of great evangelism. It will not happen among the self-righteous people; it will take place among those who have no religion found within them. We are going to see radical churches raised up in the last days because there will not be the limitations and restraints of pre-imposed traditions. People who have not been indoctrinated with false teachings and man-made religion will become the radical end-time Church.

Personally, I did not have a lot of religiosity in me to start with; but it has taken me a long time to be released from what did grab hold, and for me to be set free from the doctrines that man had imposed. That can be a great challenge, but the Lord wants us to have the liberty to break out of the old and break into the new. This is the hour of the glory and liberty of God.

As the Second Coming of Christ draws closer, we know that the presence of the Lord will become more pronounced. It will be the bridging of two worlds. We have the Kingdom and we have the earth, and as Jesus taught them to pray in Matthew 6:9-10, "Our Father in heaven, hallowed be Your name. Your kingdom come, your will be done on earth as it is in heaven."

We are seeing this transition begin to take place. The spiritual and the natural world are merging until one day, the two shall become one. In that day we will be totally consumed in the anointing and the Spirit of the Lord.

We as the Church are the vehicle to usher in the presence of the Lord. Psalm 22:3 says, "But You are holy, enthroned in the praises of Israel." As we move into this higher level of praise and worship to God, we will begin to encounter greater manifestations and anointing from the Lord. As we break through into His presence, it is in this realm that we find everything we need. His presence is the issue. We have the living Word, but the Word without the Spirit is dead.

When we worship Him, Jesus said, "God is Spirit, and those who worship Him must worship in spirit and truth" (Jn. 4:24). As we learn how to express true devotion, His presence will break through into our midst. The glory is literally the highest place of honor or admiration. Glory is the ultimate. Paul said, "And raised us up together, and made us sit together in the heavenly places in Christ Jesus" (Eph. 2:6). To be in the presence of the Lord is to behold the radiant beauty of God, to come into His splendor, and to enter into that place where everything is perfect. That is where God is intending to raise us so we will be lifted up with Him into those high places.

That is the purpose of our church services. Every time we gather together our goal is to be lifted to the highest place and to experience the presence of the Lord. It is so exciting to see what God is about to do among His people. I really believe that we are going to witness releases of His presence like we have never seen before. There will be times when the glory will come without any conscious effort on our part. God will simply make Himself known because we have chosen to abide in His presence just as Moses did.

Do we begin again to commend ourselves? Or do we need, as some others, epistles of commendation to you or letters of commendation from you? You are our epistle written in our hearts, known and read by all men; clearly you are an epistle of Christ, ministered by us, written not with ink but by the Spirit of the living God, not on tablets of stone but on tablets of flesh, that is, of the heart. And we have such trust through Christ toward God. Not that we are sufficient of ourselves to think of anything as being from ourselves, but our sufficiency is from God (2 Corinthians 3:1-5).

Here Paul is establishing sound doctrine and revealing to the people what God is producing in them. He is saying that there is something being birthed in their hearts. The Word that is coming forth out of them is not knowledge or understanding that is gained by the carnal mind, but it is a word that is being revealed from the heart. And that is how God wants to speak on the earth today. When God speaks through you, people will not want to hear what you know; they will want to hear from God who is within you.

The Spirit of God is writing His Word upon our hearts, and we are becoming living epistles to be read and known by all men.

Who also made us sufficient as ministers of the new covenant, not of the letter but of the Spirit; for the letter kills, but the Spirit gives life. But if the ministry of death, written and engraved on stones, was glorious, so that the children of Israel could not look steadily at the face of Moses because of the glory of his countenance, which glory was passing away, how will the ministry of the Spirit not be more glorious? For if the ministry of condemnation had glory, the ministry of righteousness exceeds much more in glory. For even what was made glorious had no glory in this respect, because of the glory that excels. For if what is passing away was glorious, what remains is much more glorious. Therefore, since we have such hope, we use great boldness of speech— unlike Moses, who put a veil over his face so that the children of Israel could not look steadily at the end of what was passing away. But their minds were blinded. For until this day the same veil remains unlifted in the reading of the Old Testament, because the veil is taken away in

Christ. But even to this day, when Moses is read, a
veil lies on their heart (2 Corinthians 3:6-15).

Those who are bound by tradition and doctrines of men have a veil lying over their heart. They do not have ears to hear what the Spirit of the Lord is saying. Because of the hardness of their hearts, they are not flexible to receive the anointing of the Lord. The Lord is able to break that barrier down by sending His anointing to liberate the captives. He sends His power to deliver us out of the place where we lack understanding, where we cannot see, we cannot hear, and we cannot perceive. We have lost the vision of what God has called us to be—joint heirs with Him in Christ Jesus! Romans 8:16-17a says, "The Spirit Himself bears witness with our spirit that we are children of God, and if children, then heirs—heirs of God and joint heirs with Christ."

The Lord is executing such a new move upon the earth that the natural mind cannot comprehend it. What God does next will be so far removed from that which we have known in the past that we will not know how to identify it. This can be compared to the traditional Orthodox Jewish establishment who did not recognize Jesus when He came to the earth and manifested as the Son of God. John 1:11 says, "He came to His own, and His own did not receive Him." Why? It was because Jesus was so radically different than what they were expecting.

Many churches in this hour do not foresee what is about to take place. They are not expecting the manifestation of the glory. Nor are they expecting visible signs and wonders from the supernatural realm that we are about to be ushered into. His pronounced ways will startle the mind. "Eye has not seen, nor ear heard, nor have entered into the heart of man the things which God has prepared for them who love Him" (1 Cor. 2:9).

What we are about to embark upon is the most amazing time in history that the world has ever known. All will behold the demonstration of the presence and the power of God. Hebrews 3:3 says, "For this One has been counted worthy of more glory than

Moses, inasmuch as He who built the house has more honor than the house." If you thought the Book of Acts was exciting, wait until these last days when the presence of God is poured out in fresh waves upon the earth! "And it shall come to pass in the last days, says God, that I will pour out of My Spirit on all flesh" (Acts 2:17a).

Believers are feeling the anointing in and on their flesh because we are moving into new and different atmospheres. I do not believe in emotionalism, or anything that has an "ism" attached to it. I also do not believe in hyping and conjuring up feelings, because they can be deceiving. But I do believe that when the anointing comes, it will get right into our emotions, right into our flesh, and we will have emotional and fleshly experiences; but you must first start out in the Spirit. What is birthed in the Spirit is what we are looking for, and what God is anointing in the Spirit is what is being birthed in this hour. That is the treasure we are seeking.

These are exciting days when the Lord is elevating this whole process and unveiling His glory upon the earth. I never dreamed, some 30 odd years ago when I started in the ministry, that I would see and hear the things that I am witnessing today. The presence and manifestation of the Lord as we are experiencing today is beyond description. If all of this were to stop now and we do not partake in anything more of what we have been experiencing, 20 years from now we will look back and say, "Those were the days when the glory was here."

But we do not want an "Ichabod," where the glory departs. We must continually cry out and invite His presence and all His fullness into our midst. Our heart's desire is to become the temple of the Holy Spirit. When the children of Israel were coming back from Babylonian captivity to restore the temple in Jerusalem and they found all of Jerusalem had been ravaged, they not only rebuilt the wall but also rebuilt the temple. The temple symbolized the habitation of God. It was the place where the anointing would abide, and the people would not rest until they could once again return to where the glory dwelt.

And that should be our heart's goal in our churches. We want to establish a dwelling place for the Lord where He can come as freely as He chooses and anoint us as He wishes; a place where He can be all to us that we desire and even more. His gates will be gates of praise and His walls will be walls of salvation. The glory of the Lord has risen upon us, and all men shall see His glory radiating from us. They will be drawn to it like a bug to light.

The glory that comes will release us from the fear that once bound us. We will be like those in the Book of Acts when the anointing and power fell and the boldness of God came upon them. They were consumed with love and boldness. When the glory breaks through, it chases away the demons of fear, anxiety, frustration, and futility. The glory chases away the inadequacies of our human nature and brings the strength of God to bear witness upon our lives so that, "If you can believe, all things are possible to him who believes" (Mk. 9:23).

Get ready, for the day is coming that whatever you say shall be done. Jesus said, "And I will give you the keys of the kingdom of heaven, and whatever you bind on earth will be bound in heaven, and whatever you loose on earth will be loosed in heaven" (Mt. 16:19). There is the Kingdom authority that accompanies the glory. The power is not in who you are or what you have achieved. The power and ability to do all things in Christ is accomplished by the transformation that takes place in us when we enter into His presence. We are seeking this marvelous glory so that our lives will be changed. The glory will magnify Jesus and the Father.

> *...I saw the Lord sitting on a throne, high and lifted up, and the train of His robe filled the temple* (Isaiah 6:1).

In our church when we see the glory cloud, I think it represents the train of God; it is as though the Lord is passing by. We ask, "Where are You, Lord?" And He says, "Here I am." Some people say, "No Lord, I don't want any more. Give me less because if You give me much more I'll be ostracized, and my church members and my neighbors and my parents won't understand me. My children won't understand me, Lord, so please don't give me too much of this. I don't want to get too radical and act like Bill Hart."

I have learned what it is when Paul said that he became a fool for Christ (see 1 Cor. 3:18, 4:10). Do you realize that God is not one bit concerned about your so-called dignity or respectability? He is not interested in making you look good; His desire is to shine through you so that He may be glorified through your life. So just abandon yourself and quit worrying about what other people are thinking. Just go hog-wild for God!

Jesus said, "Seek, and you will find..." (Mt. 7:7b). Hunger after the Lord. Hunger, hunger, hunger, because the depth of your hunger determines the level of your experience. Some say, "But I don't want any of those experiences! They tell me at church we are not to have any experiences." The Lord will go through every church, and He will put a sign on some that says, "Glory Barn," and on others, "Funeral Home." Do you want to go to a funeral on Sunday morning? Galatians 2:20a says, "I have been crucified with Christ; it is no longer I who live, but Christ lives in me." We are alive in Christ! The anointing is here!

Do you know that if you will turn to God today, something spectacular will happen in your life? How long will it take for God to touch you? Not long. How far away is He? Not far. Deuteronomy 30:14 says, "But the word is very near you, in your mouth and in your heart, that you may do it." How quick can God meet your need? In the moment of a twinkling of an eye you can be transformed, radically changed into something that is totally opposite of what you might be today.

I am a candidate to be changed into something different. I don't necessarily like being the same today as I was yesterday. I want to have a fresh anointing each new day. When one turns to the Lord, the veil that prevents us from seeing clearly is removed. How quickly the Lord can break our deception! How quickly He can break off whatever is holding us back. He can do it in an instant. Jesus says in Revelation 3:11a, "Behold, I am coming quickly!"

The purpose of God manifested through His Son, Jesus, is to bring blessings to mankind. He is not interested in our twisted games or our foolish doctrines. He is not preoccupied with the thousands of different groups that say they are the only ones with "the" truth and everyone else is deceived and going to hell. God's only concern is bringing salvation and a blessing to mankind.

Jesus said, "Most assuredly, I say to you, he who believes in Me, the works that I do he will do also; and greater works than these he will do, because I go to My Father" (Jn. 14:12). And how is that accomplished? It will not happen because we venture out on our own. Only by working jointly together as a many-member body can we see His will done on earth as it is in Heaven. That is how God is to release and multiply great works upon the earth.

God's purpose of placing His Spirit in you is not to please you; it is to please God. This is not about you saying, "Well, I want to go find a church that meets my needs." No, you are supposed to be at a place that meets His need. Our heavenly King's desire is to be worshiped and glorified. Psalm 45:11 says, "So the King will greatly desire your beauty; because He is your Lord, worship Him."

We are not here to say, "I want to be somewhere where I am comfortable." We are here to magnify the King of kings and the Lord of lords. We are here to worship Him with all of our heart, our mind, our strength, and our soul. It is not about your comfort. In life, if you live in a comfort zone, you will not ever go out of your house.

Jesus said, "Follow Me, and I will make you fishers of men" (Mt. 4:19).

"I've got to leave everything to do it? Is that what You are asking me, Lord?"

"Yes."

"I've got to leave father and mother and houses, and all that I own to follow You, and then You'll make me a fisher of men?"

And the Lord says, "That's right."

"Okay, let's go!"

And what do you gain? You gain everything. And the degree of your intensity to God will determine the degree of His intensity ministered back to you. A lot of people are expecting to receive something, but they never do because they never give.

God's intentions are to always give and bless and multiply for that is His heart. He freely pours out His blessings to the world, giving His salvation to humanity. He graciously stretches forth His compassionate hand to touch the whole earth with His presence. God has commissioned us as ambassadors, as perfect representatives of the Lord. We can go to the world and say, "Behold, I've come in the name of the Lord. I've got a blessing and I cannot contain it."

So we spread the wealth, spread the glory, and spread the anointing, for whatever God has given you He has also given you the ability to share. And the more you give, the more He will pour back into you.

The key to releasing the blessing of God is that we reach out and begin to touch someone with the hand of the Lord. That may mean touching an area where no one else will go. Not many of us want to go into leper colonies, do we? But it is symbolic of what Jesus wants us to do. He gave us an example in His own life during His earthly ministry. Jesus boldly entered into the infectious colonies and extended His healing touch to those who were facing physical death.

He wants us to go to the areas in people's lives where no one else has gone before, to find the areas of defeat, to find the areas of lack and need, and to be able to bring the anointing of the Lord right into their situation and heal in His name. That is the Balm of Gilead that bears His presence to the wounded soul.

And how do you touch someone with His presence? It's not hard. You just say, "Lord, use me as a vessel to touch others with Your presence." Become an infectious carrier of the glory. If we really begin to do this, what an awesome revival and visitation we could have in our cities! If we would begin to bring the glory to people, how radically transformed our cities could be.

Our cities, towns, and communities will never be transformed by religion. The churches that have been built by the hands of men will never save them. Only a small percentage of people are even responding to God in any form or fashion. I could go out in the area around my church on a Sunday morning, canvass the whole neighborhood, and I'd be lucky to find ten percent of the people in church. Most of them are mowing their lawn, shopping, vacationing at the lake, etc.

There is nothing wrong with mowing your lawn, shopping, or going to the lake. But only a small percentage of the population of our cities has the desire to be in church. Why? They are looking for something more than what has already been given to them. When God begins to manifest, He does not want to reveal Himself just in your church, He wants to manifest in the whole city and state and across the nation. He wants to make Himself known throughout the whole earth. But it is up to us to become carriers of His presence and begin to speak the words of life.

The Bible says in Proverbs 18:21a, "Death and life are in the power of the tongue." You have the power to speak into people's lives an anointed word that will liberate them. One of the greatest ways to reach out is to lift other people up, to esteem them more highly than yourself, to bring them into the place of glory. That is what the Lord did. He humbled Himself and became obedient to death on the cross, and because of His humility, God lifted Him up and exalted Him. In His exalted position, Jesus reaches down and pulls us right up to be seated together with Him in heavenly places.

What a marvelous Savior we have! The Lord gives us a vision of what we can be. He always puts a vision before us saying, "This is what I've chosen for you; this is what you can become in Me." He never leaves us as orphans or as strangers, but always includes us in His purpose and His plan. We are part of the household of God, and we are the children of the Lord with a destiny in His Kingdom. He wants to increase this revelation within us so that we will walk with a clear sense of purpose.

Life is pretty meaningless unless we have a purpose in Christ; for what kind of life would it be just to live and work and have a family and then die? There is much more to life than that. There can be a lot of fulfillment in family, friends, and careers; but the real calling on our life is to glorify the Lord and to ultimately be a part of His Kingdom forever.

Second Corinthians 3:16 says, "Nevertheless when one turns to the Lord, the veil is taken away." This is such an awesome Scripture. And in verse 18 it says, "But we all, with unveiled face, beholding as in a mirror the glory of the Lord, are being trans-formed into the same image from glory to glory, just as by the Spirit of the Lord." What image are we being transformed into? The image of Christ!

The Lord is replicating Himself within us so that we can have the mind of Christ, and so that we will be perfectly joined togeth-er as one man, with one heart, with one faith, with one baptism, all speaking the same thing. We are to become the perfect repre-sentation of Christ here on earth. In the Book of Acts, after they had crucified Jesus, His enemies thought they had rid them-selves of the radical until they realized that Jesus' Spirit had been duplicated within each one of His disciples. They must have said, "Oh my, what have we done? We killed one, but now we've produced an army."

The Bible says that the people took note that the disciples had been with Jesus (see Acts 4:13). They knew that the disciples had been with Him. Wouldn't it be nice if you were out somewhere and somebody said, "Hey, you've been with Jesus!" And how would they know that you've been with Jesus? The same heart that is in

Him will be evident within us. The same love and compassion, the same concern, the same power, and the same authority will be manifested through our lives. And we will not speak on our own, but as the One who sent us.

It is not what we have that we give, but what we have "in the name of Jesus Christ..." (Acts 3:6b). I do not speak by my own authority; I speak upon the authority of the One who sent me. There is something awesome in you, something *dunamis* (dynamite) within you. Christ is within you, and He is the hope of glory for the whole earth (see Col. 1:27). He is ready to be revealed in us and manifested through us.

Once you get this, it will revolutionize your way of thinking because all of a sudden you realize that it is not up to you. It takes out all the fear, doesn't it? Based on my past experiences, I have many reasons to be afraid. Because I have been rejected and hurt, a lot of fear can potentially well up within me. But if I step out in the power of the Holy Spirit, then it is not me walking, talking, perceiving and speaking. It is Christ in me, and that gives me all the confidence and boldness in the world.

I can pray for someone and say with boldness, "In Jesus' name be healed; in Jesus' name come out of her!" And what if it doesn't happen? Well, it does not make any difference because I am speaking as of the Lord. It is His responsibility, not mine. I am just a representative of the Lord with the authority of God resting upon me.

"Now the Lord is the Spirit; and where the Spirit of the Lord is, there is liberty" (2 Cor. 3:17). The Lord wants to set us free into the glorious liberty of the sons of God. Jesus said, "Therefore if the Son makes you free, you shall be free indeed" (Jn. 8:36). Quit holding back. If you are going to be in freedom, be in freedom. If you are going to be in bondage, be in bondage. If you are going to be in religion, then go and stink it up in religion. If you want to be in the liberty of the Holy Spirit, then jump right in; the Holy Ghost is waiting.

How long are you going to be stuck between two opinions? How long will you live in the flesh and try to walk in the Spirit? You cannot do both. You have got to get on one side or the other. Just jump into the Holy Ghost, into the lake of glory, and start swimming!

I am one of the most inadequate people in my church. There is no sufficiency in myself to get up in front of the people and try to teach the Word of the Lord. I am just an old West Texas farm boy. I don't have anything to offer in and of myself. I know that my life is not 100 percent everything it should be, and you are probably saying that about your own life. The sufficiency I have is not of myself, but is in Christ. All I can hope to be is a vessel that He can manifest His glory through.

And that is what God wants you to be, just a vessel with an open heart to Him. Prioritize your life; set yourself, your affections, and your desires upon the Lord. He will let you have a lot of good times, a lot of fun. God is not a prude like some people portray Him to be; He is a God of liberty and freedom and joy.

If Christ is free, then we are free indeed. Do not be entangled again with the yoke of bondage. Galatians 5:1 says, "Stand fast therefore in the liberty by which Christ has made us free, and do not be entangled again with a yoke of bondage."

Accept His freedom and His presence. If you would like to have a special anointing touch from the Lord, a healing for your body, restoration, whatever you need; ask for it and accept it by faith in Him. If you want to take the plunge and get right into the Holy Ghost, it is time to do it. Just say to the Lord, "I'm tired of living on this line between bondage and freedom. I want to step over and be in the glory cloud." There is freedom, joy, and peace in the Holy Ghost waiting for you. This is the moment to do it.

CHAPTER 10

The Glory Ministry

Our whole life is tied into the manifested presence of the Lord, for without His presence and apart from Him we have nothing. The ministry of the tabernacle is a time of soaking in the presence of God, beholding the presence of the Lord, and a time of being transformed into God's image. Part of that transformation is what takes place through the mechanism known as faith, for when faith is birthed in our hearts, it becomes the launching pad to the next step that we are about to take. It is impossible to move forward without faith, because by its very definition, the activity of faith requires motion to fulfill its destiny in our lives.

In every new stage and each new step that we proceed with, God creates an increase of faith in our hearts. "So then faith comes by hearing, and hearing by the word of God" (Rom. 10:17), As God speaks and His revelation begins to birth within us, faith begins to rise up to meet the challenge of moving forward in the direction that God has prepared for us.

As we progressively walk with God, we not only attain liberty but we also find fulfillment. The more aggressively we move with God, the greater the amount of provision He supplies to us. The abundance that is provided assists us to advance in our Kingdom's calling. If He has called us, He will equip us.

A generous portion of anointing is poured out and enables us to do the will of God. We know the anointing that God grants is not wasted but has a distinct purpose. Isaiah 61:1 says, "The Spirit of the Lord God is upon Me, because the Lord has anointed Me to preach good tidings to the poor: He has sent Me to heal the brokenhearted, to proclaim liberty to the captives, and the opening of the prison to those who are bound."

In our church we have experienced the awesome cloud of glory in our midst, and there is a reason behind the manifestations. God is preparing us to move into a greater measure of fulfillment and to break through into higher realms of glory. The ultimate goal is to break through entirely into the total freedom that God has provided for those who love Him.

One time when I was playing golf, there were deer romping all over the course. It was the most unusual experience. Right when we would try to drive the fairway or hit onto the greens, the deer would begin walking across them. It reminded me of the freedom that God brings. Here we had deer in the midst of humans, their enemies, yet they were fearless and possessed absolute freedom. And that is how God brings the liberty to us; in the midst of the enemy, in the midst of our captivity, there is a liberty and a freedom that comes. We are immune from fear and shame. We do not have to hide because we have been clothed with power from on high.

Second Corinthians 4:1 says, "Therefore, since we have this ministry...." What ministry? It is the ministry of "where the Spirit of the Lord is, there is liberty" (2 Cor. 3:17). That is something that we are excited about because when the anointing comes, it strengthens our hearts and our faith and resolve. It reveals to us and shows us the reality of His presence in our midst.

When we have the knowledge of God in our midst, it brings great boldness and confidence. Sometimes when I leave the church on Sundays I feel like I'm flying or walking on water, because the presence of the Lord has been so powerfully manifested to me. When the anointing comes, we become strong in the Lord and in the power of His might.

So we have this ministry, and as we have received mercy we do not lose heart. It goes on to say in Second Corinthians 4:2, "But we have renounced the hidden things of shame, not walking in craftiness nor handling the word of God deceitfully, but by manifestation of the truth commending ourselves to every man's conscience in the sight of God."

Hindrances that once constrained us melt away as the anointing freely flows and is manifested. We have a different approach in this gospel than we did in the old-time religion that we were formerly exposed to. We are not here to preach down at people or to condemn someone for their sin. We are here to exalt the Lord. In the midst of that, sin tends to fall away.

We are not focusing upon what we are not, but we are focusing upon what we can become. As we do that, there is a transformation that takes place. If you ever try to focus on the negatives to create a positive, your outcome will be a false positive. So you must concentrate on the positive. It is by the grace of God we are saved, so set your eyes on His grace and mercy and love that is extended to us; and in the midst of that, the hidden things, the deceitful things, the things that are corrupt in our lives are taken away. We are simply replacing that which is corrupt for that which is righteous.

This is known as the principle of displacement. When we confess our righteousness through the blood of Christ, then unrighteousness is commanded to flee. The more we abide in the light, the less darkness we will encounter. We do not look into the darkness to try to find light; we look towards the light to find the light. Many people get that backwards in their approach to the Lord. The Lord is not concerned about what you are not; He wants you to be concerned about who He is.

We want to be "looking unto Jesus, the author and finisher of our faith" (Heb. 12:2a). When we look unto Him, we are transformed from glory to glory and from image to image, and we begin to radiate the very nature of Christ. I heard a preacher recently on television saying, "By the time I get through with my message, you're all going to be squirming in your seat; I don't care how righteous you think you are."

Well, you know, I don't really think that is the approach God takes. His intent is not to get us to squirm in our seat, but to have us rejoice in our faith and rejoice in the glory of God. Sure there is sin, but sin is not the focus; the focus is the Lord. It is easy to preach about what we are not; the difficult task is to proclaim our position as the righteous heirs of God's Kingdom. Our negative thoughts can build up a barrier in our mind that prevents us from laying hold of the vision of who we are in Christ.

But when God illuminates our minds and understanding and we begin to acquire the vision of how He sees us, that is the greatest revelation we can receive. God's acceptance and forgiveness brings us out of the pit, out of disobedience, out of sin and into the fulfillment that He has planned for us. We have this ministry of the glory, this ministry of liberty; and in the midst of this, the hidden things are being renounced. We are no longer walking in deceitfulness or craftiness, but now the manifestation of the truth is in our midst.

And what does the truth do for us? It sets us free. But the gospel is "veiled to those who are perishing, whose minds the god of this age has blinded" (2 Cor. 4:3-4a). If we are in this process of perishing, we are blinded and not able to see the revelation, the manifestation.

The Father sent Jesus, the Word, and He became flesh in our midst. "But as many as received Him, to them He gave the right to become children of God" (Jn. 1:12). But most reject Him, don't they? The key was not so much in what He said, or what He did, but the key was in who He was. "Unless you eat the flesh of the Son of Man and drink His blood, you have no life in you" (Jn. 6:53b).

We are not just looking to find a word from God or for Him to give us an instant remedy. What we are looking for is God Himself. The revelation of the Lord takes away the blindness. The revelation of the glory removes the deceit in our life, and the manifestation of the Lord dispels the god of this age. The goal of the god of this age is to blind people to the revelation of the Lord. He will give us a dose of religion and a dose of this and a dose of that just to keep us away from God's presence. His presence is the preeminent issue in everything that we are. Acts 17:28a says, "In Him we live and move and have our being!"

Our church is called the Cathedral of Praise because God inhabits or is present in the praises of His people. I saw in a vision that one day there will be perpetual praise taking place inside the Church, a ceaseless worship unto the Lord, so that His presence can continually be manifesting.

We can be a great people, with great kindness and generosity; but more than having a sense of who we are, we pray that the people who come to our church will experience His presence in our midst. The God of salvation is the only gift we really have to offer mankind, and it is only through Jesus His Son, that true transformation can come into their lives.

The ministry God has given us is founded in faith. We come in faith to obey God; we come in faith to believe God; and we come in faith to enthrone the Lord in our midst. Second Corinthians 4:4-5 says, "Whose minds the god of this age has blinded, who do not believe, lest the light of the gospel of the glory of Christ, who is the image of God, should shine on them. For we do not preach ourselves, but Christ Jesus the Lord, and ourselves your bondservants for Jesus' sake."

And that becomes the primary emphasis and the crux of our message—to exalt the Lord. Jesus said in John 12:32, "And I, if I am lifted up from the earth, will draw all peoples to Myself." The message does not consist of "how to" theories or "why to" philosophies. Nor is it motivated by, "We hope to...." The message is: "Jesus Christ is Lord, to the glory of God the Father" (Phil. 2:11b). That is the revelation we seek.

We must continually reject the plans of men that attempt to make this gospel complicated. We simply say that all we are to do is to lift up Christ. It is the simplicity that is in Christ Jesus. Paul said in Second Corinthians 11:3, "But I fear, lest somehow...your minds may be corrupted from the simplicity that is in Christ." Do not depart from the simple message that Jesus Christ has been crucified, buried, and is risen to the glory of God the Father.

We accept the crucifixion of Christ and that He shed His precious blood to cover our sin, but that is not our focus. We accept that we are buried with Him in death, but again that is not our focus. Our primary focus is to rejoice in the resurrection and the coming of the Lord. He lives! He is seated at the right hand of the Father, and our eyes are always focused upward, seeking Him, not looking to that which is below. We are not recalling the former things, but we are calling out to that which is to come. This focus keeps us out of the bogged-down and worldly position that will eventually bring us into ultimate destruction.

We can say "Yes!" and "Amen!" to the promise of the Lord as we press forward in this hour, strengthening our resolve and determining that we will not lose this battle. And we must not quit. We will fight the good fight of faith that has impregnated our very being. Faith is growing so strong within us that we too will be those who step out of the boat and begin to walk upon the water.

We also will be those who speak and it shall be done unto us according to His good pleasure. We will be the ones who enter into complete agreement with one another and together we will witness God command His blessing out of the mountains of Zion. We know that, "faith is the substance of things hoped for, the evidence of things not seen" (Heb. 11:1).

We, the true believers, sons of God, the Bride of Christ, have reached into the unseen world and called those things as not as though they were, and our faith has increased to the point that we can begin to expect anything to happen. "Eye has not seen, nor ear heard, nor have entered into the heart of man the things which God has prepared for those who love Him" (1 Cor. 2:9). We can literally begin to expect breakthroughs beyond our comprehension. Faith is being birthed and is growing strong in our hearts as we come into the presence of the Lord. This faith is causing us to become someone greater in Christ than what we could have ever imagined.

We are not preaching ourselves, but Christ, and proclaiming that we are servants of the Most High. We are here as stewards of God, set in the house of the Lord to be the channels that He can manifest Himself through. God is saying that this is our ministry, and it is not what we are, not what we are able to accomplish, or what accolades we can achieve in this life; it is simply that we are the vessels the Lord is choosing to show up in. And He shows up in spite of us!

None of us are worthy to carry the glory or to behold God's presence. Not one of us has merited enough favor with God for this to happen, but it does because of His infinite grace. We have learned to position ourselves properly so that His grace flows freely through us. Grace is coming to us, and grace is going from us to reach the earth. Jesus said in Matthew 10:8, "Heal the sick, cleanse the lepers, raise the dead, cast out demons. Freely you have received, freely give."

That which God is birthing in our church and in other churches around the world is going to manifest to the whole earth. The knowledge of the glory is going to break through like a shining light in the darkness and go forth in Jesus' name. "For it is the God who commanded light to shine out of darkness, who has shone in our hearts to give the light of the knowledge of the glory of God in the face of Jesus Christ" (2 Cor. 4:6).

Every time you connect with the Lord in worship there is a light that begins to beam out of you; the light then shines forth from you. I have experienced this recently as our worship on Sundays has gone into higher and higher levels. It is as though there is light radiating towards us and then reflects from the people in our church. "Arise, shine; For your light has come! And the glory of the Lord is risen upon you" (Isa. 60:1). I love this glory because it is in the glory that we find wisdom, and all things join together to equip us to become what we are called to be in the Lord.

As we please Him with worship, God commands this light to shine out of the darkness. It pleases God for you to worship Him in spirit and in truth. We are not coming to worship at a mountain or a shrine or a temple; we are coming to worship Him in spirit and in truth. In the midst of the worship, the glory is manifesting. Second Corinthians 4:7 says, "But we have this treasure in earthen vessels, that the excellence of the power may be of God and not of us."

If you want to see God do something special, just continue worshiping Him. He will take away your disbelieving heart and bring you into a place of great faith. As we worship and break through the restraints and barriers, we are coming so strongly into His presence that we can taste His presence and His glory, taste His anointing and grace in our lives. Psalm 34:8a says, "Oh, taste and see that the Lord is good." And in Psalm 42:1, "As the deer pants for the water brooks, so pants my soul for You, O God."

Just as the thirsty deer pants for a drink of water, we yearn for the Lord and to be in the courts of God. The old covenant priests had their seasons of yearning. During the Feast of Tabernacles, they would build a tent and dwell in the booth for seven days. They called it the tent of meeting because that is where God promised He would meet them. And our cry becomes, "Lord, let us be met in our churches in our 'tent of meeting' and let us encounter the manifestation of the presence of the Lord!" Second Corinthians 4:10 says, "...that the life of Jesus also may be manifested in our body." What a fulfillment that is! That is the glory of the Lord.

> *Therefore we do not lose heart. Even though our outward man is perishing, yet the inward man is being renewed day by day. For our light affliction, which is but for a moment, is working for us a far more exceeding and eternal weight of glory, while we do not look at the things which are seen, but at the things which are not seen. For the things which are seen are temporary, but the things which are not seen are eternal.*

For we know that if our earthly house, this tent, is destroyed, we have a building from God, a house not made with hands, eternal in the heavens. For in this we groan, earnestly desiring to be clothed with our habitation which is from heaven (2 Corinthians 4:16-18, 5:1-2).

We come to worship God and we confess, "Lord, I have no clothing of my own; I have nothing of myself. What I receive today, let it come from Heaven. Clothe me, oh Lord, with Your robes of righteousness." We come empty-handed, not commending ourselves, not bragging nor esteeming ourselves higher than we should. But we come groaning with a desperation that cries out, "Lord, whatever we are to be, let it come from You because what we have is perishing." What we have is temporal and corrupt, but what the Lord has is eternal and righteous and glorified.

We are exchanging this old man for the new man that God is creating in us. His renewal is transforming our inner man into a brand new creature. Renewal and glory has begun to enter into the house of the Lord once again. I don't know what is in store for us, but I believe there will be breakthroughs into the next realm that will be so pronounced that you will see and hear things that no living creature has ever witnessed before.

Let me give you an example from our own church. One Sunday morning we heard thousands of voices and instruments. It was the most awesome sound! Out of our little crowd there was a magnificent cathedral and an awesome glory that was just spinning in the air! We were breaking through into a heavenly realm. It reminded me of the time I broke through in 1973 and heard the angelic hosts. Once you break through into realms of glory, suddenly the whole atmosphere becomes charged with worship in the presence of God. It is a phenomenal experience.

God's glory is coming because we have desired His presence with everything that is within us. The psalmist writes, "One thing I have desired of the Lord, that will I seek: that I may dwell in the house of the Lord all the days of my life, to behold the beauty of the Lord, and to inquire in His temple" (Ps. 27:4). Verse 6 goes on to say, "And now my head shall be lifted up above my enemies all around me; therefore I will offer sacrifices of joy in His tabernacle; I will sing, yes, I will sing praises to the Lord." Worship of the highest level is birthed out of the deepest hunger and an uncompromising determination to break through. We press in with a hunger for God, and we continue to press in for the breakthrough until the manifestation comes.

We believe, as Jesus said, "Where two or three are gathered together in My name, I am there in the midst of them" (Mt. 18:20). The Lord is in our midst, and the higher we lift Him up and the more we proclaim His glory, the greater His glory is revealed. "If indeed, having been clothed, we shall not be found naked" (2 Cor. 5:3). We do not want to be found naked; we want to be arrayed with glory.

> *For we who are in this tent groan, being burdened, not because we want to be unclothed, but further clothed, that mortality may be swallowed up by life. Now He who has prepared us for this very thing is God, who also has given us the Spirit as a guarantee. So we are always confident, knowing that while we are at home in the body we are absent from the Lord. For we walk by faith, not by sight. We are confident, yes, well pleased rather to be absent from the body and to be present with the Lord* (2 Corinthians 5:4-8).

We use the above verses at funerals, but this Scripture is not referring to death. True, if you are six feet under and you are absent from your body, your spirit is present with the Lord. But Paul is describing an active and living scene, which is perpetually taking place. We are absent from this body, this consciousness, this reason and thought, while we are in the presence of the Lord. When we are self-contained in the natural man and trying to approach God in the flesh, we are then absent from the Lord.

It is only when we abandon our flesh and self-will and come up out of ourselves completely that we will be found in the Lord's company. If you are contained solely within yourself, you will never experience His divine presence. But when you come up out of yourself your spirit can then begin to soar and rise up to meet the Lord in the air. Now that is an out-of-body experience! You must crucify the old man with its affections and desire in order to become a proper worshiper.

You say, "I refuse to let this old man assert his will. I crucify my own to do the will of God. I crucify my selfish thoughts and self-determined mind-set, and I come up out of this old man and into the mind-set and the presence of God." And that is a revelation, isn't it? To be absent from the body is to be present with the Lord. It doesn't mean to physically keel over and die. You are dying to the old man and coming alive in the new.

> *Therefore we make it our aim, whether present or absent, to be well pleasing to Him. For we must all appear before the judgment seat of Christ, that each one may receive the things done in the body, according to what he has done, whether good or bad* (2 Corinthians 5:9-10).

We are coming into His presence with thanksgiving in our hearts, rejoicing in the Lord. He is birthing a ministry of liberty, glory, reconciliation, and revelation; a ministry of light that is shining out of the darkness and coming forth in the midst of the house of God. We give Jesus Christ the honor and glory as Lord, and we are filled with eagerness and anticipate all the manifestations of His presence in our midst.

CHAPTER 11

The Glory Prepares Us

At the end of Moses' life, the nation of Israel was prepared to enter into the promised land. After they wandered 40 years in a wilderness, the Lord was ready to fulfill the promise He had made to Israel's forefathers—a land flowing with milk and honey.

Moses announced during this time of transition, that he would not be crossing the Jordan River with them. He explained that Joshua was now their commander in the Lord's army. God's new leader emerged, clothed with fresh anointing and power, equipped to usher an entire nation into the next level.

The principle of provision is enacted in every aspect of our walk with God. When the Lord pours out fresh anointing, His people are transported into greater and higher levels. During this process, God properly positions and sends out those who are called to do His will.

Joshua possessed a unique anointing because of a deep hunger to know the Lord. Moses, Caleb, and Joshua continually sought God's face in the midst of their wilderness experiences, because they knew that to overcome daily challenges, they would have to seek the guidance of One greater than themselves. While in the desert, they obediently erected a tabernacle for God to inhabit. Joshua and Caleb would tarry in the tent of meeting after Moses left to rest. They desired more of the Lord, and determined to saturate themselves in the glory. God faithfully prepared His children before promoting them to carry out the demanding task ahead.

He knows the day will come that we will face situations and challenges beyond our ability to cope, strength to endure, and faith to believe. Have you ever reached a point in life when everything appeared to be coming up roses and then suddenly, a monkey wrench was thrown into the equation and your world turned upside down? I believe that you overcame the odds because the Holy Spirit prepared you beforehand.

God is preparing the Body of Christ for awesome days ahead, but also, days that will hold her greatest challenges. The days will be exciting and filled with great manifestations, not only in the supernatural realm but also in the physical realm. Where sin abounds, grace abounds much more.

One morning while showering, I was thinking about my business, KingsWay. My showers are sometimes quite long because I am so caught up in my thoughts. While I was contemplating how good it is to have such a wonderful company (KingsWay is debt free, money in the bank, and business is cruising along fine), I realized God required something greater. The Lord challenged my heart as I sensed Him saying, "I am now ready to take you to the next level."

I went to the office, and I didn't give the word I received any more thought until later when I opened a package. Enclosed was a complimentary book. When I saw the title, it jumped off the cover and into my heart. The title was: *Good to Great: How Companies Go From Being Good Companies to Great Companies*, by Jim Collins. The opening sentence said, "The greatest enemy of greatness is goodness."

I was faced with an immediate challenge, knowing the Lord was saying that I must not take ease in Zion while there is still a mission ahead. At once, I recalled Israel's history and how the Hebrew children took a passive position in the wilderness. After forty years of God meeting their every need, they had developed a dependent mind-set. It took the surge of a fresh anointing to deliver them from their wandering plight.

After all, it is not so bad to be in the wilderness when you have a cloud by day, fire by night, manna every morning, and your shoes never wear out. Granted, the landscape is a bit stark, but it is easy to depend on God and grow lazy. However, God had other plans.

Joshua was called to break Israel out of her passivity. Although Israel had falsely assumed life would remain the same and they would never have to face another trial, Joshua became empowered by God and would lead the people through the upcoming challenges, including encountering giants in fortified cities.

The minute you step out of the boat and into faith is the very moment life's greatest challenges will be there to greet you. The moment you believe God for something greater is the moment the enemy will throw you a curve.

> *Beloved, do not think it strange concerning the fiery trial which is to try you, as though some strange thing happened to you* (1 Peter 4:12).

The same Spirit who was in Joshua must also be in us if we expect to advance and conquer life's giants. God's fresh anointing breaks the yoke of the past, and His great power ushers you into the next level. Truly, a land before us is flowing with milk and honey. "Eye has not seen, nor ear heard, nor have entered into the heart of man the things which God has prepared for those who love Him" (1 Cor. 2:9). The Father has prepared blessings for those of us who love Him, that are beyond our wildest imaginations.

God has an awesome Kingdom for us to inhabit, but we are required to take the next step, and the next and the next. Nevertheless, venturing into unknown territories can be terrifying. All our life preservers and ropes, whatever we have held onto in our own strength, must be cut loose. Whatever could pull us back to safety, "just in case things don't work out," is no longer an option. Cut away all your lifelines and declare, "I'm either going to sink or swim!"

> *And Peter answered Him and said, "Lord, if it is You, command me to come to You on the water." So He said, "Come." And when Peter had come down out of*

the boat, he walked on the water to go to Jesus.
But when he saw that the wind was boisterous, he
was afraid; and beginning to sink he cried out,
saying, "Lord, save me!" And immediately Jesus
stretched out His hand and caught him, and said
to him, "O you of little faith, why did you doubt?"
(Matthew 14:28-31)

Put yourself in Joshua's shoes. Before crossing the Jordan, you "had it made." You now face danger because of the uncharted lands you are entering. Your company has never come up against such mighty cities; not a soul with you has been there before. You must begin to advance, entirely by faith, realizing there are no other options. Once you cross the river, once you make the commitment, there is no going back. On that day, the manna ceases. Suddenly, God deals with His people on a different level.

The Lord may be saying to you today, "Your manna is drying up and you are going to starve if you stay where you are." No wonder the law of diminishing returns is taking place in your life. The Lord is prompting you to jump in and cross the river!

I know, beyond a shadow of a doubt, if I had not heard the voice of the Lord in the shower that day, and had not taken an initial leap of faith, all that I had settled for would have simply vanished. Even though I was happy and at ease, God would not have allowed me to live in my comfort zone any longer.

If you suddenly find yourself homeless, you must find somewhere else to live in a hurry. The Lord is saying, "Be ready. I am going to do something brand-new. Fresh anointing will break through and suddenly you will begin to move into something awesome."

Every place that the sole of your foot will tread upon
I have given you, as I said to Moses (Joshua 1:3).

God does not honor a "que sera, sera ,"—"whatever will be, will be" attitude. If this attitude is in you, expect the worst to happen.

God gives us His promises, but His Word is not effective unless someone trusts and obeys. See His Word fulfilled as you declare, "Yes, I believe God's Word and promises are true!" Amen.

The Book of Joshua reveals Scriptures that are essential for claiming victory. God instructs us to claim His anointing and promises through faith, before His Word is fulfilled in our situation. "Have I not commanded you? Be strong and of good courage; do not be afraid, nor be dismayed, for the Lord your God is with you wherever you go" (Josh. 1:9).

Fear can paralyze and prevent God's people from moving forward into the next glorious realm. Many of us are afraid of leaving our comfort zones, but we must be careful; whatever our greatest fear is could be what tries to destroy us.

The Lord told Joshua,

> *This Book of the Law shall not depart from your mouth, but you shall meditate in it day and night, that you may observe to do according to all that is written in it. For then you will make your way prosperous, and then you will have good success* (Joshua 1:8).

Do you want to be successful? Then believe the Lord for prosperity and success. Also cast out fear and let the courage of God rise up in your heart. Soon after I received God's challenge that day in the shower, it was confirmed out of the mouths of witnesses. I began to take steps immediately, yet there are many future steps ahead.

A wonderful example of God fulfilling a promise was back in January 1987. Our church moved into its present building with little income and a lot of faith. Our total offerings for 1986 were less than the monthly building payments we were about to incur. It appeared as though we were putting ourselves in jeopardy. What did it take to make the move? It took courage. We could not be afraid nor focus on what would happen if our financial obligations were not met. To forfeit all the church had worked for would have been devastating.

The good news—God blessed us the following year with tithes and offerings, which tripled the previous year's. Today we can report that our church is in the home stretch of becoming completely debt free. Only by faith are we able to obtain God's promises. "But without faith it is impossible to please Him, for he who comes to God must believe that He is, and that He is a rewarder of those who diligently seek Him" (Heb. 11:6).

God will not allow you to move into a place where everything is neatly lined up. You must have faith and courage to believe God, even when it seems as though the Lord is holding back His provision. Numerous times, I have stepped out in faith and sank down to my neck. I would convince myself that God had abandoned me. Only when I lost *my* strength and could not hold on any longer did His hand reach down and lift me up.

I began to step out in faith, standing on God's promises for KingsWay. Shortly after, a gentleman called early one Saturday morning. I was half awake when the phone rang and looking at the number, I realized it was an associate in Canada. I assumed he was about to share a negative report, because of the challenges we were facing at the time. I'm glad I answered the phone, because, much to my delight, he said he had never been this excited before becoming a part of our company, and he believed something awesome was about to happen in his life.

"All of a sudden," he said, "my enthusiasm and everything within me that has been dormant these last few months, is now bursting forth. I'm sharing with as many people as possible! I have meetings lined up six days a week for the next six weeks! I believe now is the time to put my hand to the plow, because there is a great harvest coming!" While he was talking, I was thinking, Thank You, Jesus. The steps I took could have literally put us into bankruptcy. Instead, new associates are joining us on a daily basis and

KingsWay continues to flourish. Praise God. After taking these steps of faith, the confirmation of the Word came to me. If you cast your bread upon the water, the bread will return, and the breakthrough is inevitable in Jesus' name.

I don't know your situation, but I believe this applies to you as well. I believe God is saying to us, "I want you to have courage in this hour. I want you to step out where you have never gone before, speak where you have never spoken, hear things you have never heard, and see things you have never seen. I'm ready to do something mighty in your midst. You cannot lean upon your own understanding, but you must lean upon the salvation, anointing, and the power that comes from on high." The Lord is saying we are to prepare to enter in.

Past provisions will not suffice for what we need for the future. God instructed Israel to prepare earthly provisions before crossing over into the promised land. Now, the Lord is advising the Church to prepare spiritual provisions for His future Kingdom. We do not want to be identified with the five foolish virgins who refused to prepare. When the day came to meet their Bridegroom, the door to the wedding feast was shut to them. They lacked provision. They lacked anointing. At the last minute, they were out shopping for oil to fill their empty lamps. (See Matthew 25:1-13.)

Only those who have been soaking like sponges in God's presence will be prepared to enter into what God has set before them. I wonder what my life would have been like had I not prepared myself all these years, to hear His voice, to recognize confirmations, and to be led daily by His Spirit. Where would I be?

I certainly would not be in the promised land flowing with milk and honey, but more likely lost in a spiritual wilderness, wandering to and fro. Without the Spirit's anointing and courage, the giants I encounter in my life would surely intimidate me from moving forward with God. Only the Lord's strength, power, and anointing breaks the yoke of the enemy. When His anointing comes, fear and intimidation must flee. Amen.

Saturate and prepare yourself to enter into the next level. We cannot fathom what God will do when we remove all the self-imposed limitations and allow the anointing of the Lord to be our strength and guide. "For as many as are led by the Spirit of God, these are sons of God" (Rom. 8:14). I like being a son of God; it is better than being a son of the devil. I like being on the right team, at the right place, at the right time, because that is where I meet the glory and the power.

I am anticipating something awesome happening as God leads me to the next step. I dream about it at night and think about it during the day. There will be future church services where no telling what could happen! The glory might come with great magnitude, the angels of the Lord might appear, and Jesus might return! Hallelujah! I do not know what to expect, but I will believe, as long as it takes. I have preached this word for a long time, and I'm going to continue preaching it, because I believe it. Amen.

Prepare yourself, get ready; it is time to celebrate the "feast of trumpets." The time has come to sound the alarm: "Prepare the way of the Lord" (Mt. 3:3).

There are many more hard battles to fight, and yet I have never been of much worth if I have not been fighting a devil or two. God puts that tenacity in us. As followers of the Lion of the tribe of Judah, we have within us a God-given spirit to go forth and conquer. We are not to be like those who bite and devour one another, but we are called to fight the good fight of faith, continuing to battle, until we lay hold of the word spoken over our lives.

I cherish the Spirit's anointing and the liberty that God offers. "But those who wait on the Lord shall renew their strength; they shall mount up with wings like eagles, they shall run and not be weary, they shall walk and not faint" (Is. 40:31). When we wait on His Spirit, the anointing will come to strengthen and immerse us into the river of God. Let us go down to the river and be baptized in His glory!

Set yourself to do the will of God and do not hold back. Do not be limited and do not limit Him. Let God be all He desires to be to you. It may not happen immediately, yet it could. What is happening in our church now did not happen overnight. It began in 1984, when I first moved to Austin. I began an early morning (6:00 a.m.) prayer meeting in a small Baptist church. Three teenagers and I would come to pray each morning, but it was not long before the enemy attacked and put an end to the prayer meetings.

Soon after, I was called to establish our existing church. Again, we began meeting every morning at 6:00 a.m. to pray. We met in a rickety old building on Highway 290, complete with broken heaters and lack of insulation. During the winter, the wind would blow in from the north and creep in under the door. The chill would pierce us right to the bone.

Donna Triplett, Billy Turner, and others would come to pray. From 1985 to1993, we arrived at 6:00 a.m. and prayed every morning. Nine years of dragging myself out of bed at 4:30 a.m. to get there at 6:00 a.m. because of the long drive into town, just about killed me. Each morning after prayer, I would also broadcast a live radio program, and that too, just about killed me.

Then God called us to do something more—Friday night prayer meetings. Our church has been interceding every Friday since that time. God's signs and wonders that are appearing before us are not by accident. The manifestations are here because we have been crying out for more of God—more of everything and anything that God chooses to impart. We believed that no matter how long it took, we were going to hang in there until we had the fullness of His presence. The same Spirit who quickened Jesus' mortal body from the dead will also quicken us. Then we will be glorified together with Him.

The glory of the Lord is so good, so awesome. Do not take your ease in Zion, living in your luxurious houses, while the house of God lies desolate. Submit your self wholly to Him and commit completely to His will. His glory is waiting.

I have been committed to preach for the past 30 plus years. Over half of those years have been in our present church, and I continually cry out to God, because I have beheld His glory. Once we taste of the heavens, how can we go back to being earthly minded? Once we taste of the glory, how can we be satisfied with the temporal? I can become as earthly and temporal as anyone; however, there is something of eternity in me that continues to cry out. So I keep returning to the house of God, because within His walls there is glory, hope, and salvation. I know Jesus is coming; the full manifestation of His presence is at hand.

The last days ahead are magnificent, and as we behold Him, we will be transformed from glory to glory and from image to image. God is preparing us for the promised land and for the fulfillment of the Word. Do you want to be a part of His Kingdom? Do you want to be engaged in fulfilling God's destiny? Is your desire to be a part of the Church who makes history and breaks through into realms of glory, which the world has yet to see? The opportunity waits, because the Lord is ready to pour out His anointing on those who trust and believe His Word.

People who have come to our church searching for a perfect pastor have always left sorely disappointed; however, those searching for Jesus have found Him. Jesus is in the house and He loves our church. He has found worshipers here who have a heart for Him—people who love and have a great hunger for Him. We are not boasting about who we are; we glory only in the things He is in us.

God has shown His pleasure and we believe that is why we have experienced a cloud of smoke during services. God has affirmed our praises with these signs. Supernatural smoke. Have you heard or read about such things? Many in our church have witnessed this on more than one occasion.

Something special and awesome is stirring in the heavens. How can we ignore these signs and be like the unbelievers who say, "Oh, it was just a puff of smoke" ?

God is sending His wonders, and yet, if we do not participate and embrace them, then who are we? Are we dead? When a sign comes such as this, it represents something very special happening within the Church. Something beyond comprehension is about to take place in the life of the Church. I keep praying, "Lord, don't let me grow so accustomed to Your presence that I begin to take Your glory for granted."

If all the signs stopped tomorrow, it would not make a difference to me, because my heart has been strengthened by His presence. I am beginning to feel like Superman!

> *He who is in you is greater than he who is in the world* (1 John 4:4b).

I feel like I can leap over tall buildings, run faster than a speeding bullet, and stop a speeding locomotive with my bare hands.

> *If you have faith…nothing will be impossible for you* (Matthew 17:20).

One of our church members, Dora, was talking to a woman and telling her about the glory manifesting in our church. The woman came back with a curt remark, "Well, I don't have to follow after signs and wonders." She said this as if we were deceived. Dora had the foresight and wisdom to reply, "Neither do I, because when you're a believer, signs and wonders will follow you."

We all have heard someone say, "Have you heard about what God is doing over at that other church?" We too, probably thought, You've got to be careful about those signs and wonders—they can deceive you. But now, all I can say is, "God, show me more, because I've never loved You as much as I do now. I've never had as many tears flow as I do now; my heart has never been as melted. My vision and faith have never been as strong as they are today."

Run to the glory! "Lord, pour out the extra portion on us that nobody else wants. Everything they reject and don't believe in, then please give us their share!"

There are times when human nature is utterly ridiculous. Man foolishly states, "I don't believe in this," or "I don't believe God is in that." We should never question what the Lord is doing! It is not our business. He is God! God can do just whatever He desires. He has never said, "I want your opinion on whether I am God or not," or, "I need your opinion on what I should do." God is under the distinct impression that He is God!

Be not deceived; God is not mocked (Galatians 6:7 KJV).

Just what does God want to do? He desires to bless His people, super-abundantly, above all we could ask or think. What is God going to do? He is preparing to pour His glory out on humanity. "In the last days, says God, I will pour out of My Spirit on all flesh" (see Acts 2:17). The Bible describes the signs and wonders that all of creation shall behold. The manifested presence of the Lord is revealed to strengthen and encourage the believers.

Keep your ears open; God is talking to His people. If your ear is trained to listen to what the Spirit is saying, rest assured, that is His voice. Then when a fly-by-night word is spoken, you will discern the difference. Jesus said, "My sheep hear My voice, and I know them, and they follow Me" (Jn. 10:27). When God speaks, He does not take you from point A to point Z all at once. He takes you step by step, from point A to point B and so forth.

When a nominal Christian comes to me and says, "God told me that tomorrow I'm going to be an apostle to all of Africa," I know that isn't God talking; it is their ego. However, if someone comes to me and says, "God told me to clean the church toilets," then, I am more likely to believe them. When you first begin as a humble servant, then you position yourself to become an apostle to all of Africa.

I was saved and called to preach while I attended a small church in Amarillo, Texas—Hillcrest Baptist Church. At that time, the people were in the midst of a mighty revival. Pastoring was Brother Frank Ryecliff, a praying man who loved God. He was a down-to-earth Baptist preacher, like myself. Brother Frank had a heart for the Lord, and in a couple of years, that small church became one of the most dynamic congregations in the Southern Baptist Convention. During those years, as I recall, Hillcrest ranked third in number of baptisms throughout the entire denomination.

Within six months, approximately 35 young men at Hillcrest believed they were called to preach. The church abounded with preacher boys, and all possessed ambition and visions of grandeur for their ministries. Many times young preachers naively assume God has called them to be the next Billy Graham. All they see before them are throngs of people being saved, television appearances, best-selling books, and the accolades that follow the life of a successful evangelist.

I was a little different. My heart was greatly humbled that the Lord had called me. I did not position myself on the front row like most of the young preacher boys. Sitting up front with their finger in the Bible, they anxiously waited for the preacher to call on them. They waited a long time. That was his pulpit, not theirs.

Out of that group of young men, as far as I know, I am the only one still preaching. I volunteered to do whatever needed to be done at the church. My first assignment was to minister to the seventh-grade boys' Sunday school class. It may have seemed like the least desirable place on the planet, but gladly and gratefully, I submitted. I wept at the opportunity to minister to those few boys and teach them about Jesus.

Immediately after the boys were dismissed from class during the week, they met me out in front of the school for snacks. I was then privileged to lead them in an after-school Bible program. My heart was broken at the chance to share Jesus with them, to have the opportunity to give them God's Word. Although I questioned, "Is this where I'm supposed to be?"—less than a month after I began teaching the seventh-graders, invitations to preach began to arrive. Only eight months after being saved, I was pastoring full time.

I learned an important principle during that time of humble beginnings. Those aspiring preacher boys did not volunteer to serve God with a contrite heart. They were ambitious and sought recognition and a prominent position. I cared nothing about that; I only sought to become a servant and love the Lord.

I am here today, not because I was the most talented. I wasn't. Nor was I the most qualified. No—far from it. The only reason I remain in the ministry today is that God's presence constantly reminds me of the humility of Christ, His greatness, and who we can become in Him. There is nothing like it. Isn't the Lord wonderful? I believe He is here with us. How can we describe His glory? How can we relay the feelings we have for the Lord?

At times, I feel like an old man; but when I am in God's presence, I feel like a child again. I remember experiencing my first taste of glory around the age of eight. One day, as I was playing in the front yard of my home in Muleshoe, Texas, the glory of God came on me. I remember looking up into the sky and feeling His love for the first time. Now when I enter into His presence, I am again reminded of the time when the God of Heaven reached down from the sky and touched me.

Sometimes, eight-year-olds today are not so innocent. In Muleshoe, back in the '50s, there was a lot of innocence. I was a naïve little boy with a pure heart, and when I enter into God's presence today, I feel the same way. My past mistakes and sins do not weigh me down because I am in His presence, His love, and His joy.

Oh, how I appreciate the Lord today. How much I thank Him for His mercy. I end up crying at the end of our church services. I think the older I become the more I cry. A few years ago, I never would have dreamed that we could experience the glory the way we do today. I was willing to serve God the rest of my life without these experiences. And if I never feel His touch again, I would love Him because my heavenly Father has given me incredible blessings...*enough to last a lifetime.*

For additional resource material from the author, contact:

Bill Hart Ministries

Cathedral of Praise
3406 Tarlton Lane
Austin, Texas 78746

512-328-4522

www.copaustin.com

Additional copies of this book and other
book titles from DESTINY IMAGE are
available at your local bookstore.

For a bookstore near you, call 1-800-722-6774

Send a request for a catalog to:

Destiny Image₀ Publishers, Inc.
P.O. Box 310
Shippensburg, PA 17257-0310

*"Speaking to the Purposes of God for This
Generation and for the Generations to Come"*

For a complete list of our titles,
visit us at www.destinyimage.com